DOGS
IN
ACTION

DOGS
IN
ACTION

Working dogs and their stories

MARIA ALOMAJAN

First published 2013

Exisle Publishing Limited,
P.O. Box 60-490, Titirangi, Auckland 0642, New Zealand.
'Moonrising', Narone Creek Road, Wollombi, NSW 2325, Australia.
www.exislepublishing.com

National Library of New Zealand Cataloguing-in-Publication Data
Alomajan, Maria, 1970-
Dogs in action : working dogs and their stories / Maria Alomajan.
Includes bibliographical references.
ISBN 978-1-927187-99-9
1. Working dogs—Anecdotes. 2. Hunting dogs—Anecdotes.
I. Title.
636.70886—dc 23

10 8 6 4 2 1 3 5 7 9

Text design and production by IslandBridge
Cover design by Christabella Designs
Printed in Shenzhen, China by Ink Asia

To the selfless human volunteers and all the phenomenal dogs in the world who excel at jobs which serve humans and to which they are devoted until the end, my deepest and most sincere gratitude. Thank you.

Beauty without Vanity,
Strength without Insolence,
Courage without Ferocity,
and all the virtues of Man without his Vices.

Epitaph to a Dog (Lord Byron)

Contents

Introduction

Dogs are the only species on this planet which lives and works with humans in such a deep, meaningful and all-encompassing way.

My first experience with a working dog was with a very handsome German shepherd named Kurt. Actually, Kurt was a failed police dog so wasn't really a working dog – he wasn't up for the serious stuff, but he was our awesome family pet.

Although he didn't pass police academy, clearly Kurt's tracking training had worked because he would either follow us to or find us at school (the only dog belonging to any of the hundreds of children at our primary school who did such a thing). I only wish at the time I had known what that meant, but instead I was always embarrassed to be called in by the principal – again – to take Kurt home at lunchtime. I can still see him waiting by the fence at the bottom of the sports field.

He was the focus of endless search and retrieve missions, as many an early morning would see pyjama-clad humans cycling the streets calling for the runaway dog who had escaped, seeking a bitch in heat. On one occasion he even crashed through a plate-glass window to embark on a procreation mission!

Kurt drank from the toilet bowl, found our missing cats, stole the neighbour's Sunday roast, played with us, went jogging with Mum – and never so much as curled a

Kurt, still handsome as an old boy.

Jet at the beach.

lip if we stepped on or fell all over him. The only thing we remember him being afraid of was big trucks – he would freeze and cower if one went past.

He had a habit of engulfing the entire head of one of our cats in his mouth and then releasing it, seriously covered in slobber. This was a slightly disturbing sight for us, yet obviously comfortable for the two of them, as the cat – named Lucky – never stopped approaching him and he never stopped doing it.

At one stage we had five German shepherds at home – I think some of them may have been pups from his wayward travels…

Kurt was just always there. We never had any discussion about the fact he was 'just' a dog. He wasn't any different, he was just one of us, and I am eternally grateful to my mum for making this the foundation for my relationship with animals.

So that's where my love of and keen interest in working dogs started. I loved the idea Kurt could have been a police dog, but also loved it that he came to live with us instead.

A few wonderful dogs later and my current boy Jet is very cool, extremely handsome and has an awesome work drive. We have tons of fun learning new stuff all the time. I had hoped he could be a 'working dog' but he's too much of scaredy-cat to do the tough stuff, such as search and rescue, and turned out to be too much of a foodie to look for truffles. He has, however, to my surprise, excelled in front of the camera and starred in TV commercials and several photo shoots (not all my own). So that's not bad for a beaten-up, starving street puppy rescued from the wrong side of the tracks.

I love to watch dogs work. Seeing them in action, using their nose, their ears, their awesome brain – working things through, figuring things out – they are so clever, focused and driven. They read the world in a way we humans can't, communicating with us and training us in ways we still struggle with in return.

To anyone reading this book who may be in doubt, I can assure you these dogs love their jobs, they come alive when they're working and clearly thrive – and equally enjoy their downtime afterwards. As the expression goes, they work hard and play hard. Every single person I met or spoke to in researching this book reinforced to me that the work must always and forever be fun for the dogs. They also said theirs was the most handsome/ beautiful and talented dog on the planet … and each of them was right!

'The most important thing about the work we
do with our dogs is that they enjoy the work.
Bottom line.'

Peta Clarke

Sled dogs

Blaze and Arluk

At twelve years of age, Blaze has run over 40,000 kilometres (nearly 25,000 miles). An incredible feat, which seems more astonishing when you see her petite frame all snuggled up in a fleecy blanket in the back of the car or on the master bed. Looking at her it would be hard to guess that this gentle, small girl with the greying muzzle and beautiful face has such endurance, stamina and leadership skills.

Blaze is a semi-retired Alaskan husky sled dog who runs as lead dog and has completed six Iditarod challenges and four Yukon Quests.

Probably the oldest form of work for a dog is pulling a sled. Evidence of harnessing dogs for transportation dates back to 2000 BC, and archaeological evidence from Canadian Thule sites depict sleds fashioned from whalebone and sealskin.

When reviewing history, certainly sled dogs played a large role in world events such as the conquest of both the North and South Poles. Roald Amundsen, the Norwegian Arctic and

Antarctic explorer, used sled-dog teams when he successfully reached the South Pole.

Helmer Hanssen, who was responsible for the welfare of Amundsen's sled dogs on the South Polar expedition recorded in his notes: 'Dogs like that, which share man's hard times and strenuous work, cannot be looked upon merely as animals. They are supporters and friends. There is no such thing as making a pet out of a sledge dog; these animals are worth much more than that.'

As true as those words were then, they are now.

During the long frozen winter months, dog sleds were used in places such as Alaska, Greenland and Russia, where the temperatures can drop below minus 40°C with wind-chill factors of minus 70°C and where whiteout blizzards are common. Dogs were a critical part of life for a long time in these places, where they were the sole means of transporting people, mail, supplies, commerce, trade, provisions and – especially important – doctors and medical supplies.

To this day, in extreme weather conditions when the vehicles, helicopters and snowmobiles – which rendered dog sleds almost redundant – are useless, the formidable dog-sled teams are called upon again as the only means of transport.

How do these teams navigate in such dire conditions? Certainly without GPS technology. Instead teams use trail markers, if they exist, or look for landmarks (impossible in places like the Arctic) or trust the dogs to follow the lay of the land and pick their way over the snow. Lyne McFarlane, Blaze's human partner, points out that the dogs always know better than the humans riding the sleds what the snow is like underfoot because they are on it. She says: 'You can use voice commands but when you're running a big team of dogs the lead dogs are about 30 metres in front of you so they know what's going on with the snow surface and feel with their feet, see with their eyes any changes/things to avoid and they guide the whole team.' It's a big responsibility to be a lead dog and you need a super-confident and calm dog for the role – which is the position Blaze held.

Above

Blaze leads Lyne and the team during a Winter Festival race.

Left

Blaze, an Alaskan husky, takes a break.

Lyne recalls a time when she was in the Arctic doing research and Old Hippie (a lead dog) took them all on a merry dance. He was determined to visit an old camp site, which they had only ever used once, five years prior, so he just turned the team and took them there with total disregard for the humans protesting otherwise.

With what they are capable of, it's easy to think sled dogs must be big and strong, and some are, but some like Blaze and her contemporary, Arluk, are surprisingly slight – they just share the same spirit as the giant wolves who preceded them.

Sled-dog teams historically carried incredible weights over extraordinary distances. North West Company fur trader Daniel Harmon recorded on 13 December 1812: 'I have seen many dogs, two of which would draw on a sledge, five hundred pounds, twenty miles, (226 kilograms, 32 kilometres) in five hours. For a short distance, two of our stoutest dogs will draw more than a thousand pounds (453 kilograms) weight.'

The Siberians considered their dogs to be companions, protectors, hunting partners and guardians of herds of reindeer, as well as pulling dogs. Dr Robert Crane, a specialist in Russian studies, wrote that 'the combination of intense climatic variations and the presence of other hostile tribes had forced the Chuchkis to base their economy on the rapid means of transportation provided by the sled dogs, which allowed them to cover long distances on the uneven ground of the tundra and ice fields.'

And indeed Arluk, a strong, handsome Siberian husky, demonstrated his awesome power when he was one of the lead dogs in a demonstration, where 10 dogs, on their own, pulled a 12-tonne tram from a standing start. Which wasn't the plan at all, it was just that the driver had hesitated in putting on the electric power to assist them so the dogs started pulling and moving it themselves. Needless to say their booties were completely worn through and their humans – Ray and Dianne Holliday – who have the health and well-being of their dogs always at the forefront of their minds, were far from happy.

With so many films, TV shows, cartoons and stories written

15

Arluk, a Siberian husky and lead dog.

and produced starring sled dogs – *Eight Below*, *Balto*, *Sled Dogs*, *Call of the Wild*, *White Fang* and *Born to Run* to mention but a few – most people think they 'know' these dogs. But their sheer power and speed is hard to believe unless you see it or experience it in person. A few times a year, during endurance races such as Iditarod, the Yukon Quest and the International Stage Stop Sled Dog Race, sled dogs exhibit their amazing abilities for the world to see.

Although controversial because of its competitive nature, the Iditarod Trail is a re-enactment of an historical journey made in 1925 by sled dogs during a dire medical emergency. The Serum Run to Nome or Great Race of Mercy, as it is also known, took place when a diphtheria epidemic threatened the people of Nome. With no way to get the urgently required antitoxin from Anchorage to Nome except via train and dogs, that is exactly how it was done. The amazing dogs who ran that trail saved countless lives.

One of the reasons breeds of dogs such as these are so well prepared to work in these extremely cold conditions is because of the mechanics of their coats. They have a double coat, which means they have a shorter layer which traps air against the skin preventing heat loss, and a longer coat that protects against the environment and also helps with insulation by trapping additional air. This double coat acts to keep the dogs warm in winter and cool in summer. As well as the double coat, some of a dog's hair is filled with air. An elongated snout allows the air being breathed in to warm before it reaches the lungs, thus avoiding ice crystals potentially entering the lung cavity.

Sled dog breeds have bigger hearts than humans, with three

times the oxygen intake of an élite athlete and the ability to metabolise fat as well as carbohydrates, giving them access to at least twice the energy. During races like the Iditarod and the Yukon Quest, dogs can consume up to 12,000 kilo calories of energy per day, compared to an average human demand of around 2000.

What makes a good sled dog? Eric Rogers from R Northbound Dogs in Alaska defines it as: 'A good sled dog has to be an athlete first, but that's pretty much standard these days. I think a good sled dog must have a sense of adventure, a desire to explore, to

Arluk leads a six-dog team.

want to see what's around the next corner or over the next hill. There needs to be a little stubbornness so they don't quit when the going gets rough. A little pride so they don't want another team in front of them. And finally a willingness to listen to and trust their musher [the driver of a dog sled] particularly when we tell them to slow down and pace themselves because the race doesn't end in Skwentna [a stop on the Iditarod Trail].'

Blaze is a great sled dog – born to run. But unlike most sled dogs, who buck and pull and bark and howl with uncontained excitement and anticipation as soon as they know they're about to run, Blaze remains very dignified and ladylike. Some may say she's almost casual about the whole affair, as she has to be coaxed into position at the front of the team, where she then waits in a slumped sit as if to say, 'When you're ready.'

Lyne attributes some of Blaze's quiet routine to nerves, but mostly puts it down to experience. Having done what she has done, Blaze knows how and when to conserve energy, to sit tight and rest and then when to let it rip.

However, it's a different story when Lyne is ready. Then Blaze comes alive and truly is the leader of the pack, guiding both the dogs and Lyne with supreme confidence. Aside from saying the two of them have a special bond which goes beyond words, Lyne recalls '[Blaze] making a decision to take the team out of a really soft blown-in trail and onto a much better one. She does follow commands as well, but sometimes she'll know much better than me – and I guess that's the trust relationship we have in working together.'

Arluk is also a lead dog, the first dog to be attached to the gangline. Standing calm and still, holding the gangline taut, he waits patiently until the rest of the team is hooked up. When the snub is released, allowing the team to move, a change comes over him and, like Blaze, he's all business.

Commands for sled dogs are simple and few – 'mush' or 'OK guys, hup' which means go, 'whoa' which means stop, 'gee' indicates to go right and 'haw' to go left. Ray and Dianne also have 'easy' to tell the dogs to ease up a bit. The lead dog takes the verbal commands and actions them. And a sled, even with only two dogs, operates as a tight team.

With teams of three or more dogs there is a leader, followed by swing/point dogs, team dogs and, the last dogs stationed in front of the sled, the wheel dogs.

The lead dog is the most critical. As the title suggests they lead the team; they stop and the team stops. The lead dog turns and the team turns, they push on and the team will follow through the harshest conditions Nature has to offer. Lead dogs must be mentally sound as well as physically able, as they regulate the team's speed, set the direction and lead the team past any distractions. As a lead dog Blaze will turn and glare at Lyne if she tries to ride the sled up a steep incline instead of running alongside it. Lyne knows Blaze is just looking out for her team and she knows it's time for her to run.

The second most important dogs in the team are the wheel dogs. These are often bigger, stronger dogs, because the sled, if fully laden, can be heavy and difficult to move or turn. As well, wheel dogs need a calm, steady nature so the sled and its movement, so close behind, doesn't spook them.

The swing/point dogs sit behind the lead dog and guide the team around curves and during turns. Team dogs are the ones in between, who are chosen for endurance, strength and speed. Swing/point dogs are often leaders in training.

Places like Denali National Park in Alaska still use dog teams to patrol the inner two million acres of wilderness where vehicles are prohibited. The dogs are used for

Arluk and his sled team – Libby, Squirt, Kotick, Minti and Eva.

19

contacting winter visitors, hauling supplies, transporting wildlife researchers and to help ensure there is no illegal poaching or vehicles in prohibited areas.

Some people 'living off the land', in places such as Alaska and Greenland, continue to maintain the tradition of living and working with their dogs. When supplies need to be hauled, trap lines laid or firewood collected, it's done by a 'man' and his dogs.

Back in New Zealand, Arluk, the strong, proud, aloof retiree who refuses to jump, shows distain for and tiptoes around any damp grass when he has to do his business in the morning – although it doesn't bother him when he's chasing possums up the nearest powerpole – has other claims to fame. He starred in the BBC documentary *High Altitude*, and in television commercials for American company Glidden Paint and UK Nissan Navara. A dog of many talents, with distinguished good looks, he is rather like the James Bond of sled dogs. Arluk – or as he is known formally – Sibenah Anadyrs Arky, is one of those husky dogs, who for all intents and purposes, when you see him standing rooted to the ground, surrounded by snow and howling to the sky, you could swear was a wolf.

Police dogs and victim recovery dogs

Jess finds human bodies, or remnants thereof as the case may be, to assist forensic victim identification teams. Not a glamorous or enviable part of her job, but a critical one, which has to be done to give closure to the family and loved ones of the victims of tragedy.

Officer Jess is a police dog. If she could speak, at eight and a half years of age she could tell some tales to make your hair stand on end, and has seen things most dogs and humans shouldn't have to see, yet she remains a happy, enthusiastic girl. Full of life, she clearly continues to love her job.

Police departments employ dogs in a number of roles. The most common and most recognisable are 'patrol' dogs. These canines are the companions of cops around the world – highly trained dogs employed in everyday law enforcement and utilised for jobs such as the tracking and holding of suspects and crowd control. Many of them also accompany officers to schools and community groups to assist in education programmes.

As a baseline, police dogs are trained to a level of agility, tracking and obedience which is much higher than that expected of the average pet or competition dog.

After baseline training is completed, dogs which have shown a natural affinity for certain types of work will be dual-trained in specialist areas such as explosives, narcotics, firearms or currency detection, or, as in the case of Jess, victim recovery work.

What this means is that when search and rescue teams are satisfied they have completed their search for a living person/ persons, they draw a line in the sand and make a call that the operation is now a 'victim recovery' mission. Then a team such as Jess and Sergeant Salmond will be called in to find the deceased.

When missing people are suspected to have been murdered and a body or body parts may be hidden or buried, trained specialist dog teams receive a call to assist search teams.

Operational police dog continues training.

In cases of natural disasters such as earthquakes, fires, tsunamis, floods, or anywhere there are humans missing, these dog teams are also called in. It should be noted there is a distinct difference between the two parts of a mission: search and rescue teams look for the missing living, and recovery teams take over and look for the deceased. While it's not uncommon for a dog trained in one area to raise an alert, and find something for which they are not trained, such as a SAR dog finding a cadaver, this is more to do with the natural ability of the dog rather than training. And should this happen, the dog will indicate differently. This is where the close bond between handler and dog comes into play, where a handler can read their dog's body signals to the tiniest ear flick.

Officer Jess and her partner, Sergeant Salmond, have been witnesses to phenomenal tragedy during their six years working together, but it's their job and they do it well.

When Sergeant Salmond was training Jess on cadaver work after she left general patrol aged about three, he had no idea what lay ahead. He thought they would spend their time together finding a deceased tramper or the occasional murder victim. He could not have known that within nine months of becoming operational he, Jess and three other dog teams would be flown across the Pacific twice to assist in international disasters. They were called on to help with the Melbourne fires of 2009 and the devastating tsunami in Samoa the same year. Then in 2011, with what seemed little respite, they would undertake the sad work of looking for victims in their own backyard after a massive earthquake hit Christchurch.

February 2009, Victoria, Australia. The state had been experiencing a drought and heat wave, with temperatures over 46°C (115°F) coupled with winds of 100 kph (60 mph). These winds shifted during the cooler temperatures of the evening but intensified to 120 kph (75 mph), blowing down power lines which in turn ignited fires in dry lands and turned the flanks of other fires into full on fire fronts. Over 4500 km^2 (1.1 million acres) burned over a few days and 173 people died as a result.

Some of the victims had little chance of escaping, while others gathered at what they thought to be the safest place. Sadly, they were wrong, and this would be where Jess would later discover their remains.

Sergeant Salmond describes their working environment as a picture of complete annihilation, and talks about scenes where an unearthly silence lay heavily over places where once there was life.

In fires of such extreme velocity and temperature, buildings, property, and devastatingly people and animals aren't just burnt – they are incinerated. All that remains are fragments or outlines of where they were taking shelter when the fire caught them.

In traumatic scenes such as this there are two official jobs for dogs like Jess – and one less official, but probably more important. The first is to locate any person or parts of a person so forensic scientists can use what she discovers to identify victims. The human victim identification team in Melbourne was duly impressed not just with Jess's dedication – even under extreme physical stress she didn't want to stop searching – but her phenomenal ability to locate items as small as a tooth or finger. While this sounds very gory, it is of huge importance to loved ones and responders.

In one house Jess searched there was no evidence amongst the remnants of deep soot and smoldering burnt bricks, visible to the human eye, of the nine people who died there.

Her ability to work in such daunting heat in severe conditions is one of the traits Sergeant Salmond lists as a particular quality which makes Jess such an awesome dog. It would have been long and painstaking work for humans to literally shift and sift

Opposite

Jess and Sergeant Salmond assist the Australian police with recovery of the tiniest remains.

Jess waits patiently as Sergeant Salmond puts on her protective booties before they start work.

everything at the site to discover the items Jess was so easily able to find.

Whilst this is heartbreaking work for their handlers, for cadaver dogs such as Jess it is all part of a 'game', something she does to receive a reward for being successful. When she makes a find she gets to play with a tug-toy offered by her handler, which is huge fun for her. Not quite as much fun as her off-duty favourite, which is finding a massive log at a park and playing with it for hours, but it comes close.

One great thing about teams like Jess and Sergeant Salmond is that her handler knows at the end of the day that Jess is a dog, and will always be a dog, no matter how well trained. And he lets her be a dog. This is why he can only smile and shake his head when, after dressing in thick layers of protective clothing to go into the smouldering burnt-out wilderness, he looks up just in time to spot Jess in her protective booties taking off to chase a kangaroo. That's her gone for an hour. It's almost as though she knew that with all the headgear and protective mask on, there was no way Sergeant Salmond would be able to call her back to work . . . so she took full advantage of the situation. And when she returned it was work as usual, as if no time had passed.

The other side of the job is of equal importance during these incidents, and that is to 'clear' an area. A dog team or group of dog teams can clear an area in a search site within a fraction of the time it would take humans to probe, use lasers or shift by hand. Clearing an area means searchers are satisfied they have covered every centimetre and there are no victims. This means responders can quickly move on to the next area. This saves time and resources and, most importantly, lives. In an area covering thousands of square kilometres there is no comparable method for speed and efficiency than to have it cleared by dog teams.

This precise skill was critically important in Samoa later that same year, when six people were missing on the shoreline after a tsunami devastated the islands. There were at least eight kilometres (five miles) of massive piles of debris to search along a wrecked beach. It took the four New Zealand dog teams six days to clear the beach, whereas it would have taken many more people at least a month to do the same job. Tragically, the missing people were later washed ashore in another area.

The unofficial side, but possibly the most important part of Jess's job, was apparent in Kingslake, Australia. Just being there in times of distress was incredibly valuable to highly traumatised people. While Jess isn't that good with other canines, she is wonderful with people, especially children.

Families returning after the fires, with nothing left and nowhere to go, were overjoyed to see Jess and her mates. There's something about a dog which makes people feel secure, providing a comforting element amidst so much devastation and destruction. Patting and playing with this workaholic dog brought a smile to children's faces. Victims knew they were being taken seriously, with everything possible being done to find their missing loved ones. As Sergeant Salmond says: 'It's a booster for morale. We all know what they say about the chemical changes in humans when they're around dogs. Well I've seen it firsthand in a disaster scenario and I was proud to be part of a team which clearly made a difference, or at least put a smile on someone's face when they had lost so much.' And on a more personal front Sergeant Salmond says he thinks the work he has done with Jess has also made his family proud.

But it's not all doom and gloom – even amongst dire catastrophe there's some much-needed light relief.

As Jess was searching the partially collapsed cathedral where it was thought 22 people may have been missing in Christchurch after the 2011 earthquake, she indicated on some rubble. Positive no one was there, others on the team second-guessed Jess's nose, but Sergeant Salmond was sticking by his dog and encouraged further investigation. Sure enough, after digging a little deeper rescue workers discovered a tired, hungry and dehydrated pigeon, which had survived five days buried in the rubble – and was promptly named Barney Rubble. Barney became a signal of hope for the city and lifted the spirits of those for whom he was the first sign of life they had found for days.

It's their sense of adventure, drive to work, desire to succeed and stable temperament in unknown and dangerous environments which make dogs such as Jess exceptional, even amongst other working dogs. In Melbourne where the ashes and soot were knee-deep with all sorts of unknown debris, with shards of glass and razor-sharp steel ready to cut her paws, Jess didn't hesitate to forge on through where other search dogs called it quits . . . and who can blame them.

Now in her golden years, Jess is taking things a bit slower. However, when given the nod that work is available, she jumps to it like a puppy. She is so committed, focused and driven to work, there have been occasions when Jess has had to be forced to stop before her body shut down. While officially commended for the work she has done, all work and no play makes for a dull dog – and Jess is anything but dull.

Always looking for an adventure, Jess has shown she is willing to create one of her own if no one else will do it for her . . .

While deployed in Samoa the working dogs were kenneled at the consulate while their human companions were across town in less salubrious accommodation. After a long day of searching for missing people (and taking the odd swim to cool down), Jess and her buddies were fed and put to bed.

Sergeant Salmond and his fellow officers had just returned to base when a call came in that one of the dogs had staged a break-out and was partying around the property. The men looked at each other and rolled their eyes. They all laughed, knowing immediately who was creating mischief. Sure enough, upon returning to secure the dogs, the officers found Jess frolicking around the grounds having escaped her crate while the local security guards were watching from the 'safety' of the roof.

Truffle dogs

Ollie

'At the time I write, the glory of the truffle has now reached its culmination . . . the truffle is the very diamond of gastronomy . . . The truffle is not an outright aphrodisiac, but it may in certain circumstances make women more affectionate and men more amiable. Whoever says truffle, pronounces a great word, which awakens erotic and gourmand ideas both in the sex dressed in petticoats and in the bearded portion of humanity.'

Jean Anthelme Brillat-Savarin (1755–1826), French author and gastronomist, from his book *The Physiology of Taste*, 1825.

Black Diamond is the street name for the highly coveted underground fungus more commonly known as a 'truffle'. Reportedly the most expensive food in the world, a 900 gram truffle (2lb) sold for US$330,000 in 2007 and at the time of writing the price for black truffle was around US$4,000 per kilo (2.2lb) but had risen as high as US$14,500 only a few years prior. One hundred years ago producers in Italy could harvest around 1800 tonnes (2000 tons) of truffles a year – now fallen drastically to a mere 27 tonnes (30 tons), with climate change the culprit.

This scarcity and the intricate way that truffles need to be harvested have made this culinary delicacy coveted, like never before. Truffles need to be located and harvested when ripe. Because they grow underground near the roots of trees such as hazelnut, oak, beech and chestnut, they aren't visible to the human eye, and need to be smelt out by a trained dog (or pig) with a 'good nose'.

In a *60 Minutes* exposé, correspondent Lesley Stahl discovered truffles are 'being trafficked like drugs, stolen by thugs, and threatened by inferior [products] from China'. Espionage and secrecy surround the truffle world, where the black market is run by cartels and those involved operate as a tight-lipped closed society. Truffles have been stolen, the trees have been stolen, truffle hunters have been car-jacked, beaten and murdered. And disturbingly, highly valuable truffle dogs have been stolen, or even worse, poisoned by the competition. In 1997 *The Seattle Times* reported 40 deaths from targeted poisonings of specific truffle dogs in one small area of Italy in a single season.

It's therefore no surprise that Karen Drummond, the human partner of Ollie, a two-year-old truffle dog, was hesitant to disclose his skills and have them noted in a book.

Truffles cannot be genetically engineered, unlike many other foods. According to Gérard Chevalier of the National Agricultural Research Institute in Clermont-Ferrand, 'No one has ever managed to grow a truffle in the lab, without a tree.'

Trees with roots injected with the fungus can be purchased, though there is still never any guarantee they will produce truffles. In reality, truffles cannot be 'grown' at all. Truffle farmers don't plant truffles, they plants trees: truffles grow only near the roots of certain trees (evergreen oak and pubescent oak are best). Five years later at the earliest, with 10 years more likely, the farmer-hunter paces around the grove on a cold winter day with an animal— a pig traditionally, but a trained dog most frequently— able to smell buried truffles. Sometimes the pair find a lot, sometimes not. 'You can't count on truffles,' says Jean-Louis Fioc, French Truffier. 'Maybe a tree will produce and maybe it won't.'

Pigs were traditionally used to find truffles, as they didn't require training, finding them instinctively because the scent of truffle mimics androstenol, the sex pheromone permeating boar saliva. The problem with this instinctual ability, however, is that it's almost impossible to stop pigs from eating any truffles they find – putting a serious dint in the annual harvest. Pigs also tend to damage the truffle area during their digging and in 1985 pigs were prohibited from truffle hunting in Italy.

The use of dogs to find truffles is documented as far back as 1700, and possibly even further. In the past, truffle hunters would avoid light-coloured cars and pale-coated dogs which are easier to see in the dark, thus giving away the location of the coveted prize. Another change in Italian law banning truffle hunting at night has seen less prejudice against light-coloured dogs – luckily for Ollie who is a cream Sydney silkie/Maltese cross.

Ollie was a regular visitor to Karen's house. She noticed this wee boy kept busting in on training she was doing with her other dogs and appeared to have a very strong work drive and 'nose'. Being a professional trainer, Karen had seen many dogs with similar ability never reach their full potential living just as pets. As a result, she really wanted to offer Ollie a life where he was mentally challenged to use his natural abilities. She asked if she could adopt him and as soon as this was finalised she began training him in scent detection, eventually specialising in truffles.

Training dogs is something the burgeoning Chinese truffle farmers have yet to embrace. They rely on 'raking', a process of harvesting by machinery which pulls up anything it can find, including immature truffles, a practice which also destroys the land.

The Chinese truffle grows prolifically and was used mainly for feeding pigs until recently, when someone said: 'Let's feed

Ollie loves his work and eagerly awaits the next job.

the French instead.' All of this horrified the established culinary world, who regard the Chinese truffle as inferior in quality, lacking in flavour and devoid of any aroma.

So why is it in demand? One Chinese truffle company says at the bottom of their website: 'Chinese black truffle are not the same one as the black truffle from Périgord and our white truffle is not *Tuber magnatum*. However, "economy through quality" is the point.'

While that may be the idea behind sales, it hasn't stopped the falsification of labelling and an influx of Chinese truffles into France. Italy has banned their importation altogether.

It seems contrary to traditional hunting and harvesting of truffles that a Chinese company can claim: 'We can tell the farmers what it is exactly we want before they go to harvest the truffles. If they are not instructed on picking the right truffles before they go deep in the mountain, farmers usually pick all the truffles they can find, which includes very small and premature ones.'

And the Chinese farmers often harvest by using the raking system, which seems far less preferable to a dog which can pick up the scent of a truffle at well over 100 metres (328 feet), no matter its depth. Unlike pigs, they have no inclination to gorge themselves on the truffles they find, they're enjoyable to have around and, as many claimed in days gone by, you can reward them with a bit of bread, making it very economical harvesting indeed.

Ollie receives more than a piece of bread for his hard work. He has a yummy meaty treat or gets to play tug. And, if he's really lucky, his mate Rupert the English pointer is around and Ollie gets to play tug with him before reclining on the master bed for a snooze. This is considerably less messy than Ollie's favourite game, which is raiding and ripping up the contents of the wastepaper basket and distributing the spoils around the house.

Once again, dogs prove to be indispensable and worth more than their weight in black diamonds.

Service dogs and animal assisted therapy dogs

Tana and Lennox

Tana (as in Montana) loves to show you how clever he is (and just quietly, he is extremely clever), especially if there are any treats within whiffing distance – especially if those treats are bits of dried green tripe. He'll race around and turn the lights on and off or open the fridge door – he'll play ball as long as you will, jump like a kangaroo if he even thinks there's a visitor at the gate, or lie quietly watching the butterflies as they hatch on the swan plant outside.

For all intents and purposes Tana is the sweetest golden retriever 'plus' who doesn't have a bad bone in his body. He loves affection and food and playing. This very happy boy, with a gentle spirit, is so unassuming you wouldn't believe he has such a serious job . . . or two . . . or four.

Raised in prison, Tana is now a service dog to his life-companion Belinda Simpson, and has a part-time job in animal assisted therapy. So his tricks for treats are far more than tricks – they're essential behaviours learned to help Belinda. Except for the one where he throws his ball from the yard onto the footpath and then convinces a passerby he 'needs' them to throw it back, which they do, and then he does a full head swing and throws it out again for the next person. That's the way Tana likes to train humans, make friends and ensure a daily supply of human ball throwers and bringers of special treats. I told you he's clever.

Briefly, service dogs live and work with a person they are paired to for life, whereas therapy dogs go out of the home to do their work, which is usually for others not their own family. But more on that later – first of all, here's how Tana started his life in prison.

Puppies in prisons

Tana was rescued as a young dog and given a second chance at a better life. He spent the second phase of his early life as a live-in student as part of the Prison Paws for Humanity programme at Montana Women's Prison, USA. This is where his early obedience and task training took place.

Like many similar successful programmes around the world, Prison Paws for Humanity was established with a dual purpose. Firstly, as a programme to teach prisoners responsibility, patience, self-control and coping skills, as well as giving them some vocational training. Secondly, this was also a programme where puppies and dogs could be housed and trained to help people in the community.

These 'dogs in prisons' programmes are based in women's, men's, youth and child detention facilities around the world, and their missions range from taking in rescued dogs and giving them a second chance at life, something many prisoners themselves are familiar with, to training selected puppies to be assistance or service dogs.

The prisoners and dogs are taught dog obedience, task training for service dogs, grooming, health and general well-being of the dogs. So positive is the effect of the dog programmes, some

Tana and Belinda would be inseparable even if it wasn't necessitated.

prisons operate a kennel-type facility just for housing and caring for people's pets while they go out of town.

Testimonials from prisoners who have been involved in dog programmes, prison staff and third-party dog-training organisations, all describe huge benefits, with a positive impact on prisoners. Self-esteem increases, as does work ethic, and as a result prisoner behaviour improves along with their motivation. Staff–prisoner morale is boosted, with both sides learning better interpersonal skills. The outside community fosters a more positive opinion of prisoners, and people have access to well-trained dogs for minimal cost. Lastly but by no means least, many prisoners, mainly female, report that having to care for a dog and provide for its needs and maintain its well-being has given them much better skills and awareness for parenting their own children. That's huge.

So whilst the dogs aren't officially the ones working in these prison programmes, they're doing a very valuable job. And without a programme like the one Tana came from, people like Belinda wouldn't have their amazing dogs, there would be fewer service and therapy dogs . . . and the world would be a lesser place.

Service/assistance dogs

Service dogs, by definition, are dogs individually trained to do work or perform tasks to assist people with disabilities. The disabilities may be physical, sensory, psychiatric or intellectual. They are classified as working dogs rather than pets. Service dogs are known by different names but their roles are the same; for example, they are called service dogs in the USA, assistance dogs in Australia and the UK and disability assist dogs in New Zealand.

Service dogs live with the person they are working for and spend a lot of their time being a pet, hence Tana's playtime and schedule for training children to play fetch with him after school. Tana knows when the local children will be passing by so makes sure he has positioned himself next to the gate with his ball. When the children come close he grabs the ball, twists his neck and throws it onto the footpath. With Tana looking pathetic and longingly at his ball, the children never fail to pick it up and throw it back. Actually many adults also fall for this one. Then Tana will wait until the children have reached the next power-pole and with a supernatural head spin he'll launch the ball again, catching their attention and drawing them back to play with him, until finally they call Belinda and tell her they really need to leave.

By law service dogs must be able to perform three trained tasks which alleviate the effects of their human's disability, but most learn far more than three and continue to extend their working skills throughout their lives. In addition, they complete extensive training for going into public places with their human companion.

Technically Tana would be classified as a seizure response dog. Seizure response dogs (sometimes called seizure alert or epilepsy assist dogs) are specifically trained to help someone who has epilepsy or a seizure disorder, as in Belinda's case. Abana Rehabilitation is Belinda's employer, and it was through their huge generosity, after hearing her speak one day, that Belinda was able to travel to America to find Tana.

Because dogs cannot be 'trained' to detect an impending seizure, they are trained to assist following a seizure. However, many people with seizure response dogs report their dog naturally behaves in an alerting manner prior to a seizure occurring. Since having Tana, Belinda said her seizures have decreased both in intensity and frequency – something she puts down to both decreased stress from having the assistance of Tana and the positive energy she feels having a wonderful dog in her life. This is not unusual – anecdotal evidence suggests many people with these dogs experience a reduction in seizure frequency.

If a dog detects a seizure about to happen he will nudge or paw his human insistently and in a serious manner, which differs from when just asking for a pat. This gives the person time to reach their medication and if needs be, go to a safe place before they come to any harm.

Through experience with Tana, Belinda knows she has about half an hour from when Tana starts indicating until the seizure occurs and this is usually enough time to get home or at least to a place where she can sit and not be worried about falling and hurting herself and where she is away from others who may find her seizure stressful. Tana can accompany or lead Belinda to a quiet spot. 'Being able to go somewhere quiet and safe to have the seizure and then being able to carry on without huge fuss from people around is really a big deal for me.'

Having a dog like Tana also offers a huge amount of independence to people who experience seizures, something they didn't enjoy prior to having a dog in their life. Going to work, or going out simply to do ordinary everyday things suddenly becomes a possibility for them.

Not every dog can be a seizure response dog. It takes nerves of steel and a very calm, stable temperament, as seeing their human having a seizure is very difficult and stressful for most dogs. Though extremely rare, there are recorded cases of dogs dying from the stress related to their human having a seizure.

And, although many people report changes in their dog's behaviour surrounding a number of medical incidents, seizure response dogs require full and proper training from a recognised organisation. So while Tana nudges for a cuddle, drops the ball in the nearest lap or opens the drawer by himself looking for snacks, as do many goldies, dogs selected and trained to work in this field are required to fulfill stringent criteria many pets wouldn't pass. It wouldn't be fair to put them in that position. As Belinda notes: 'He's a rare and wonderful dog and I'm blessed to have him in my life!'

Belinda also has post traumatic stress disorder (PTSD) and experiences physical challenges following a coma. As a result, Tana's role with her isn't only about seizure response – it also includes mobility assistance and emotional support.

Mobility assistance dogs

These dogs are trained to assist a person with a physical disability, who may or may not be in a wheelchair. The mobility assistance dog can assist physical mobility by either pulling a wheelchair or by acting as a 'living cane' to help their human with balance or gait. They often also encourage a person to try walking more, as the person knows their dog will be there as a brace should they stumble. These dogs clearly need to be an appropriate size.

At home and out and about, mobility assistance dogs are also trained to pick up objects and hand them to their human, to make out-of-reach things reachable, to open and close doors, drawers and cupboards. Most of these dogs can perform the

One of the valuable tasks a service dog performs is to open things like the fridge.

standards tasks required of the majority of service dogs such as turn lights on and off, press pedestrian-crossing buttons and collect the mail. They can also take your socks off, bring you your slippers and help you put them on.

Outside of their home Tana dons a different working hat as Belinda's assistant. Belinda is an occupational therapist, and when she's working Tana becomes a therapy dog.

Therapy dogs:
animal assisted activities (AAA) and animal assisted therapy (AAT)

Therapy dogs are pets which have been certified by a registered organisation as having exactly the right temperament and attitude to excel at providing therapeutic comfort and affection to people in need. To do so, they must be laid-back, seek human attention and affection, and be stable in a variety of sometimes unusual situations, where there may be all sorts of medical equipment about.

Jenna Reid-Batchelor, Lennox's owner, says therapy dogs need to be 'kind and gentle'. Lennox is one of Tana's buddies who volunteers at a residential brain injury rehabilitation facility.

Therapy dogs can work in numerous places including rest homes, hospices, hospitals, mental health units, social intervention facilities, schools, libraries – anywhere there is a need. They work with the elderly, the very young, troubled teenagers, inpatients, outpatients – with anyone. They have no prejudices and, as is often the case, especially with Tana, they instinctually know who needs them the most during their visit and gravitate towards them.

Tana's mere presence has been enough to encourage and motivate a woman to get out of bed, shower and eat after many days of not doing so, when nothing or no one else could reach her. She felt it was important to be clean for Tana and asked Belinda, 'Does Tana think I smell?' After showering and dressing for Tana, she thought he might enjoy some vegemite on toast – then decided to join him in a snack.

Lennox, a handsome rednose pitbull, won the hearts of his human parents the very first time they laid eyes on him as a tiny puppy. Now he wins hearts all over town, particularly those belonging to the residents where he works. At work he uses his love of balls and playing to engage with them. By doing so, he gently motivates them to use their limbs and exercise without realising what's going on and the valuable therapy they are receiving, simply because they are having so much fun.

Lennox also teaches residents about appropriate interactions with dogs. In doing so, he is also breaking down some horribly misguided breed stereotypes and re-educating some about how precious dogs are – and that they should never be abused.

Lennox takes his job to heart and loves helping people.

Belinda finds having a dog with her at work not only encourages people to open up and speak (even if it is only to Tana) but it breaks down barriers, especially in situations where people may not want to be there. And, in situations where people may think Belinda is faking interest or that she only cares because it's her job and she's paid to, they seem to know instinctively that dogs don't fake or lie, and always accept attention and affection from Tana.

Having Tana at work proves incredibly beneficial in managing people's behaviour, both passively and proactively. He de-escalates aggression and violence simply by his presence because clients never want to see Tana upset. Some of her clients even attend volunteer work with Tana.

Belinda says: 'His presence definitely helps improve all areas of clients' functioning – physical, social, emotional and cognitive. Every day Tana is used as a motivational tool – he's a great laugh and makes people smile. Tana loves sharing the privilege of throwing ball for him – I love that he thinks he is the best thing on the planet and everyone who comes in contact with him is

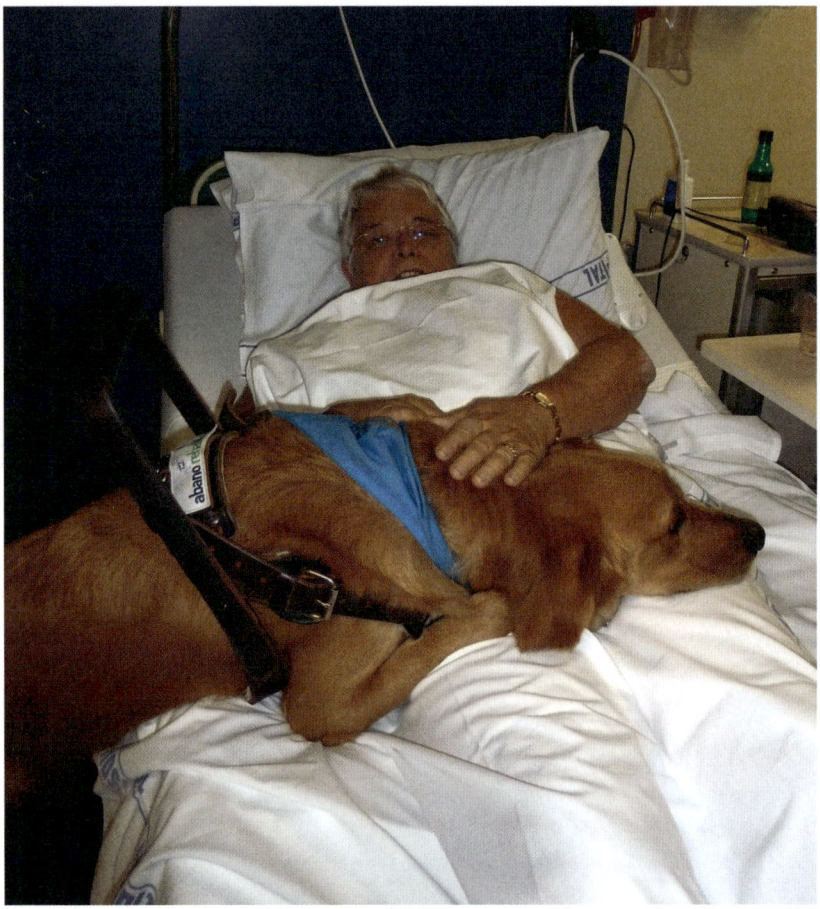

Tana knew exactly what Heather needed when she was in hospital.

better off for it. He loves to ensure that anyone and everyone can be blessed by his presence.'

But it's not just his soft coat and cool attitude that's winning people over. As Belinda is well aware, there is plenty of science behind it as well. Although studies into the effects of animals on human well-being didn't happen until the late 1970s, since then, time and time again physical benefits to humans from contact with dogs have been documented.

One of the earliest published studies in 1980 concluded people who had suffered heart attacks and owned pets lived longer than those who didn't. Closely following it was a study which found patting one's own dog could reduce blood pressure – not exactly news to those who owned a dog.

It has since been demonstrated that physical contact with dogs lowers the stress hormone cortisol, while increasing the beneficial hormone and neurotransmitter oxytocin. Oxytocin, commonly called the 'love hormone', is associated with pair bonding and maternal bonding.

Meg Daley Olmert from Warrior Canine Connection in Baltimore, USA, has said: 'Oxytocin improves trust, the ability to interpret facial expressions, the overcoming of paranoia and other pro-social effects . . . '

But it's not just humans who create oxytocin when in physical contact with their beloved dog, the dog's production of the hormone also increases. So all up there is one big happy love fest, which just has to counterbalance any stress.

Other fabulous benefits to humans from petting dogs is an increase in other beneficial hormones such as dopamine – which gives us more energy; endorphins – which create a feeling of well-being or even a 'rush' as experienced after exercise; and phenethylamine – which is associated with elation (and also found in chocolate).

Not so elating can be the off-duty antics of a wee puppy, as Lennox's family discovered. Who knew this rubbish-bin-raiding, couch-chewing Lenny Loops, aka Scooby aka Loosicles, who likes to groom and chew his dirty feet on the clean linen, would provide such crucial support to so many people in such a generous way at their time of need?

And who would guess that behind those soft eyes is a highly excitable passenger who likes to scream in delight while he's in the car? Never at work, though. Just like Tana, when Lennox is at work he's the consummate professional.

Guide dogs

Bill, Lenny, Penny and Zeke

In AD79 excavations in Pompeii revealed a wall painting of a blind man being led by a dog. Certainly the most publicly recognised job for a working dog is to be a guide/seeing-eye dog.

Guide dogs are trained to guide their blind, partially blind or partially sighted humans from point A to point B, making sure they reach their destinations safely and avoid all obstacles along the way. While the dogs are trained to travel from point to point in as straight a line as possible, they are not expected to know the directions to every destination – in other words, they're not a canine GPS system. With repeated journeys dogs often learn specific routes, but for new destinations the human partner must receive directions first, then deliver them clearly to the dog, who will then lead the way.

Their official training includes mastering two absolute essentials. The first is leading a human, who is holding the handle of the harness the dog is wearing, in a straight line. Learning to move in a straight line is essential, because it means that should the dog move out of that line the person holding the harness will instantly recognise the dog is moving to avoid an obstacle. The second essential is mastering the art of crossing roads.

Guide dogs must know how to navigate large public places and how to turn corners, take stairs and lifts and recognise changes in elevation. As well they need to know how to plot a course around smaller more private places, for example lead their person from the toilet cubicle to the washbasin in a restaurant. While working the dog must learn not to respond to distractions such as other animals, smells, noises or people, and must stand, sit or lie quietly when out with their human but not leading.

Before training begins, during training and until a human life partner is found for the new graduate guide dog, the puppies are fostered by volunteer families. These families are the full-time caregivers to the puppies and responsible for introducing them to as much of life as possible.

Claire and Mike Webb, in Perth, Australia, have been involved with therapy and guide dogs for 11 years. They have a golden retriever of their own, so the puppies are an extension to their dog family and, although Claire says, 'The hardest part is saying goodbye to them' (when they go to live with their vision impaired human companion), they continue to volunteer for this essential role. Often foster-families form a relationship with the person with whom their ex-foster lives, and they all get together to celebrate milestones and anniversaries.

Claire and Mike's current puppy is Lenny. When Lenny first moved in he was experiencing growing pains in his legs and so received the nickname Limping Lenny. For obvious reasons this name has now been changed to Leaping Lenny and the Webbs are relieved to see him turning into a normal playful pup. Prior to Lenny, the Webbs had Bill, who also provided endless joy and amusement.

Bill is now a two-and-a-half-year-old foodie. Not surprising for a Labrador. He loves fish, roast chicken and is quite partial to Morton Bay figs as they fall off the trees. Equally unsurprising is learning that food led Bill into all sorts of trouble and a rather large veterinary bill. While on a walk one day he swallowed a large piece of corncob. While no problem at the time, it later became lodged in his intestines, making him seriously ill. A very sick dog was rushed into surgery after which he remained in intensive care until he recovered. When the guide dog trainers received the vet's bill, they said, 'How much is sweetcorn these days?'

As these puppies grow up they do all the normal things – chewing up their favourite kiwi bird soft toy (pulling the eyes and wings off first); learn from the golden retriever how to dig holes in the garden; and quickly decipher the best route to take to avoid the scary cat on the corner, who stalks and attacks them.

Lenny, pup in training, sits next to Bill, a working guide dog.

Little Lenny has much to learn.

And, as part of his introduction to the world, at times Claire would take Bill into work with her. When he had decided he'd had enough and the meeting was boring, she says he would start groaning noisily or, even worse, snore loudly to make his point.

While still with these early caregivers the pups begin their job-specific training. And while Bill is an enthusiastic, boisterous young male dog who pulls on the lead and becomes very excited when he meets people, licking them on the cheek if allowed, the Webbs say he's a very different dog when he's in harness. 'He knows when he's working and needs to be on his best behaviour and when he's off-duty.' Claire continues, 'This was really brought home to us when Mike and I went on a blindfold walk with Bill just before he was matched and left home. It was amazing being guided safely along the streets by this responsible dog who was normally so cheeky and difficult to calm.'

And that is the beauty of dogs – once trained they are so earnest in their work, they remain committed for life and never forget what they have learned.

In April 2013, actor Chris O'Donnell spoke to American talk-show host Ellen Degeneres about his family pet, Kimmy, who was trained to be a guide dog but had failed to qualify due to a skin condition. She was then adopted by O'Donnell's family and he says for the first few years Kimmy thought he was blind and behaved accordingly! If he got up at night she would accompany him to the bathroom, and when out trick-or-treating for Halloween with his kids, despite all the kids and candy and excitement around her, Kimmy would walk off-lead in exactly the same position the whole time, as she had been trained. Kimmy is now 12, a similar age to Penny, another guide dog on the other side of world, now retired.

So much is seen of the cute young pups in foster care, but little is heard about older guide dogs as they move towards their retirement years. Blind sailor Vicki Sheen, physiotherapist and skipper of the winning UK blind match-racing yachting team, realised she had a problem with Penny, her elderly guide dog. 'My much loved third guide dog [is] slowly grinding to a halt. Desperate to keep me safe, she was stopping several feet short of doors and steps and walking at a speed, which unfortunately continually left me stepping out ahead of her. Doggedly determined to continue, desperately wagging her tail and pushing her head into her harness whenever it was taken up, she was faithfully trying to keep working.'

The harsh reality was that despite Penny's dogged deter-mination and faultless loyalty, her aging was impacting on Sheen's confidence to travel around the country for sailing competitions and her ability to work. With world champs and a promotion at work ahead of her, Vicki cautiously applied for another dog from Exeter Guide Dogs. Given that her colleagues wear dark suits or navy blue trousers, Vicki thoughtfully requested a navy blue dog or even a grey one with pinstripes, but for some reason, neither could be found!

For many blind people having a guide dog provides the independence they need to hold down a job, and while they may describe their canine partners as 'life savers', in the case of Michael Hingson of New York, his dog Roselle literally saved his life. Roselle led him to safety from one of the towers he was working in at the World Trade Center in New York, on 11 September 2001.

Fox News online published this on the tenth anniversary of the event. Written by Hingson, it describes the true blessing he has in Roselle and how he owes his life to his dog.

Roselle was snoozing under my desk. After the impact, the building shuddered and Roselle decided it was time to wake up. She emerged from under my desk, yawned, and quietly sat, waiting. Time to go to work. 'Forward,' I said softly. Forward is used when setting off with the dog in harness, and it's one of the very first commands all guide dogs are taught.

Roselle and I headed out of the office and navigated smoothly through the confusion, smoke, and noise.

Each tower had three stairwells. We ended up in the center at Stairwell B. Roselle was calm as ever and did not sense any danger in the flames, smoke, or anything else around us. I chose to trust her judgment because Roselle and I were a team. I clutched Roselle's harness and with focus and confidence we headed down the 1,463 stairs to fresh air and freedom.

In the stairwell, we found ways to work together to hold back panic. We were forced to stop often and we took those opportunities to encourage each other with a quiet word, a joke, or a gentle pat on the back.

Roselle did her part, giving doggie kisses to each and every firefighter who climbed past us up the stairs. Most of us in that stairwell were strangers but we trusted each other, we worked together, and we survived.

Roselle now takes her place in the history of guide dogs – an eventful history with a few hiccups and false starts, which only started in earnest when guide dogs were trained for soldiers returning from the front lines during World War I. So many soldiers had been blinded by mustard gas or suffered shell shock during the war that a German doctor, Dr Gerhard Stalling, came up with the idea to train dogs en masse to help the soldiers. The idea was inspired by his own dog, when Stalling observed him helping a blind patient after he himself had been suddenly called away from attending to the man.

In 1916 the world's first guide dog school was opened in Oldenburg, and by the 1930s there were around 4000 qualified guide dogs in Germany.

Word spread and slowly guide dog schools were established throughout the world over the past century.

Roselle takes her name from a very famous partnership in the annals of guide dog greats. Roselle Brewer, of Chicago, who became blind at the age of 20, was one of the first to receive a guide dog in the USA. One day she was listening to a radio programme when the announcer spoke about a contest where entrants had to answer the question of what they would do with one hundred dollars cash – with the best answer winning the cash. Roselle had a dead cert answer for that one – and she sent it in. She would buy a new pair of eyes, 'the eyes of a seeing-eye dog'. It's no surprise Roselle Brewer won the competition and upon applying to The Seeing Eye in New Jersey for a dog she was immediately accepted. The name of her new companion – Lady Luck.

Luck was something on the side of visually impaired Italian

radio journalist Alessandro Forlani and his guide dog Asià, when they were in Rome to cover the conclave leading to the election of Pope Francis, who chose the name of Francis of Assisi, patron saint of animals. The pair were honored to be invited into the audience hall to hear the Pope's speech. At the end of the speech, Forlani and Asià were amongst a select group of people presented to the Pope. It was on meeting the pair that Pope Francis broke with tradition and leant down to caress the dog, the same dog which had just sniffed him all over.

Also breaking with tradition, Vicki was partnered with a new male guide dog, Zeke. While all her previous dogs had been female, this boy was a leggy blond, with not a navy hair in sight. What's the difference you may ask, between male and female guide dogs?

Vicki answers that question regularly. 'Initially I didn't know, but now I've discovered the answer: when I use the ladies' facilities in a restaurant, a female guide dog shows me the cubicles, then the sinks. A male dog shows me the cubicles then whisks me straight back out of the door. He is a boy after all and boys don't need to wash their hands. When I ask a girl dog to find the car in the car park, she looks for the colour while a male dog hunts for the make and model and whether it had twin exhausts or not. A female guide dog will come up to you, snuggle in, look up at you with huge round eyes and flutter her eyelashes. A male dog will come along, cuddle up, and then belch loudly. Your female guide dog will patiently wait in the kitchen wondering if the cupboard with the chews in will magically open, while a male guide dog stays in the living room watching *Top Gear* with your husband.'

But now Vicki wouldn't be without her Zeke, with whom she says she has 'struck gold'. And to achieve such a winning combination of dog and human, Claire Webb says 'it comes down to carefully matching the guide dog's personality to the owner's lifestyle and personality. For instance a dog that's a bit

Vicki loves both her dogs, young buck Zeke and golden oldie Penny.

With Zeke at her side, Vicki is now fully mobile again.

distracted by other dogs and a little bit lacking in confidence in unfamiliar situations suits a person with some sight who is able to manage those situations. A dog like Bill, who is very active and energetic, has been matched with someone who walks a lot, goes to work regularly and is strong enough to handle him when he gets a bit excited.'

Zeke is the first dog Vicki has had who loves boats and sailing as much as she does, although he's only allowed on board when cruising. Clearly he is the perfect match. Zeke has learned to scale the ladder onto the yacht from the inflatable dinghy and knows to go from one side of the boat to the other as it tacks into the wind. He makes a fine figure, ears blown back and nose scenting the breeze, the perfect image of a salty sea dog. However, when Vicki is racing Zeke must watch from ashore with her husband. So, how does blind match-racing work? Sonar keelboats utilise a special sound system comprising three acoustic buoys, each with a unique signal to define the course.

Now fully mobile with her new dog, Vicki Sheen has regained her confidence and looks forward to travelling around the country with her new job and training hard to defend her sailing titles. During a quiet moment between races at one championship, Vicki asked her tactician, an ex-officer from the Territorial Army who used to jump out of helicopters onto roofs and break into buildings, if his old job used to be stressful. He replied 'Not as nerve-racking as spending a week match-racing with you.'

Hearing dogs

Kiri

To many people being able to hear the phone ring, kettle boiling or oven-timer going off may seem mundane and sometimes even annoying. But for those who can't hear these sounds by themselves, having a dog who can opens up their world and gives them a whole new life of independence.

A hearing dog means not having to stand by the window all day waiting for a repairman, worried you won't hear them knock on the door, because whatever you're doing, the dog will let you know when they arrive. It means not having to sit by the oven in case you burn something or wait next to the phone so as not to miss an important call – and most importantly, it frees up hours of time.

Having the security of knowing that should your baby cry your dog will alert you immediately provides deaf parents with some peace of mind. As does the early warning the dog will give if the smoke alarm goes off or an intruder is close by. This was exactly the experience of Antoinette Hartley of South Yorkshire in the UK and her five students.

Antoinette is a teacher who is accompanied to class every week by her hearing dog, Viva. The story, proudly retold by Hearing Dogs for Deaf People (HDFDP) in the UK tells how Antoinette was supervising her students, who were listening to their online course through headphones, when Viva started to alert to a sound.

Antoinette recounts, 'I was expecting her to tell me the phone was ringing as usual but she dropped straight down at my feet indicating the fire alarm was going off. The hearing learners in the room hadn't moved at all and I realised they couldn't hear because of their headphones. So I had to get their attention and escort them out of the building safely. I was so proud of Viva because she hadn't just alerted me but the five hearing learners as well and I made a big fuss of her after we got outside.'

Kiri loves getting out and about with Celia.

Hearing dogs are trained to recognise all sorts of everyday noises and to respond to the noise by alerting their human companion. They may do this (alert) by positioning their body in a certain way or by pawing. However for more serious situations such as a fire alarm going off, the alert is different, as Viva demonstrated. In these situations the dog will lay down at the feet indicating something serious needs attention.

Celia King of Auckland, New Zealand, has a hearing dog called Kiri. 'Her most important job as a hearing dog is to wake me up in the morning. She hears the alarm going off and paws the bed to let me know it's time to get up. Then she demonstrates her enthusiasm for a new day (or is it the promise of breakfast?) by worming her way towards me and encouraging me to get out of bed. Who can be grumpy when they're woken up with furry cuddles and doggy kisses?'

Kiri is Celia's second hearing dog, and she is training the dog herself after her first dog, Tara, passed away suddenly with

a heart attack, while she was chasing balls and swimming at the beach. Losing Tara was soul-destroying and left Celia heartbroken, but she feels as if Tara chose Kiri to be her next dog, because Kiri was born the day after Tara passed away.

Aside from the dogs being a practical help around the house, many people with hearing dogs attest that they feel more socially comfortable once they have a dog, and that the dog assists with employment, independence and confidence.

Not just a pretty face, Kiri is a practical help around the house too.

A case in point is that of an elderly lady in the UK, Brenda Wood. When Brenda's husband died in 1987, she lost not only her life partner but her life's 'ears' as well.

Despite her initial reservations about having a hearing dog, Brenda was quoted in October 2011 as saying: 'It's Sloe's [her hearing dog] presence that allows me my independence, but he has also allowed me to have someone else in the house as he alerts me the moment someone comes to the house. It is that love and concern beyond the expected and the understanding he has of my needs that makes him so special and such a valued companion.'

Celia King also says of Kiri that: 'She gives me confidence when I'm out and about, alerting me to what is going on around us. As she is such a beautiful dog, she gets a lot of admiring looks and comments and she initiates conversation with lots of people, which I'd feel hesitant to do if I was on my own.'

Kiri is a golden collie, which is a cross between a golden retriever and a red border collie, and Celia attributes Kiri's intelligence and her beautiful long coat – the reason she draws a crowd – to her breeding.

Being such a confident dog, Kiri takes most things in her stride, whether it's going up escalators, riding on cable cars or walking through crowds of people, so boarding a plane is a walk in the park so to speak. Having a hearing dog allows Celia to confidently fly from Auckland to Wellington each week for work (yes, Kiri has her own share of frequent flyer miles).

It was the mid-1970s in the USA when the first dogs to assist the deaf were trained, and it wasn't until almost a decade later that Europe followed suit, with Australia and New Zealand adopting the idea in the 1980s and 1990s, respectively. Today there are also training centres and dogs working in this capacity in Asia.

Celia has had Kiri since she was eight weeks old and, aside from training her to be her assistance dog, Celia also takes Kiri for therapy visits to a rest home. 'Kiri is a loving, sensitive dog and will go and comfort children if they cry,' says Celia. 'And she will lay her head on peoples' lap for a pat. Her tail-wagging and enthusiasm is infectious, and she often makes us laugh by her facial expressions, as if she understands everything we say.

'She fits so beautifully into my life and keeps my stress levels low through her work, her unconditional affection and her sense of fun. I wouldn't be without her.'

Guard dogs

Jip

Possibly one of the most coveted dog jobs in the world, these canines get to hang out with their best human buddies all day and go home with them at night, and really don't have to expend too much energy in the process.

It's commonplace to see a dog on a building site. And while it may look as though they're just lying around watching the world go by, they are in fact highly valuable, tax-deductible security assets of the business.

Jip is a case in point. Jip is a shared-custody British bulldog Staffordshire bull terrier cross, who spends much of his working day guarding tools and expensive materials at the front of a building site while Justin Walker, one of his humans, and his team are busy working around the back. Justin knows only too

Opposite
Justin makes sure Jip can get up high so he has a better view over the building site.

60

well the cost of not having a dog at work and losing all his tools. In a recent incident Jip had been hanging out in the back of the van when his other humans turned up to collect him. Shortly after Jip left, Justin's van was broken into and all his tools were stolen. Not only was this a huge financial loss in itself – the tools of his trade had gone.

Building sites can be busy places, with lots of tradesmen and subcontractors coming and going. Potentially this provides an ideal environment for someone with bad intentions to snoop around. Having a guard dog like Jip onsite has proven to be a deterrent to any would-be thieves, and he also provides an early warning system if anyone comes onto the building site.

Jip's getting older now and spends more time at home in the city or on a family farm in weekends. At 13 years of age he's greying, and while his body's slowing down a bit, his mind definitely isn't. He's a very smart dog, so don't think for a second he doesn't know what's going on around him. Off-duty Jip is just as astute and reactive. He knows when he sees his humans coming down the drive to immediately jump off the sofa and onto his own bed and pretend to be asleep . . . well partly asleep and partly guarding the house, of course.

While having a dog at home, in other words a pet, is not tax-deductible, in many countries such as New Zealand, Australia, the UK and the USA, there are tax exemptions for some working dogs. In an online article titled 'How to Claim Pet Care as a Tax Deduction', Juniper Russo writes '... [if] you own a working animal of any kind, you may be able to deduct its care expenses from your self-employment taxes. To qualify as a business deduction, the animal must be used primarily or exclusively for working purposes, such as drafting, herding, or guarding.'

Just by looking at Jip's face you know this is a dog with stories to tell – looking at his body you know this is a dog who loves his food. Apparently he's not fussy . . . except when it comes to olives. He doesn't like them and spits them right back at you.

One of Jip's favourite pastimes is being left in the car with a box of doughnuts. He knows why he's been left there and he

Standing guard at the gate, Jip boosts morale and entertains everyone on site.

commits to them as surely as he commits to watching those new weatherboards and copper drainpipes at work. Rest assured when the humans return they will barely receive any acknowledgement as he peeks at them from the corner of his eye, hiding his sugar-coated muzzle out the window.

Perhaps it's the left-over sugar the cows love, or maybe it's just because he's such a cool, calm dude, but whenever Jip is on the farm he goes and hangs out with the cows. Not in a traditional livestock-guarding way. Rather he sits with them and they gather around and all start licking his face. Perhaps he reminds them of an ancient cow god, or perhaps he's just tasty. . .

It's not just the cows with whom Jip has a rapport. He and the farm cat have an interesting bond. Status seekers by day, they will sit and stare each other out, whereas by night they become close collaborators, when they team up and go hunting together, doing a little pest detection and eradication. Watch out, possums.

A jack of all trades, this guard dog cum pest controller cum livestock relationship manager, is best known and loved on the building sites. By his mere presence, Jip not only provides security, he provides unlimited entertainment, boosts morale and selflessly cleans the floor after the team have had lunch.

And where did Jip get such an unusual name? After his humans had negotiated his adoption with some people from out of town, they discovered after a long drive to collect him that the adoption fee had doubled – they'd been jipped!

Avalanche rescue dogs

Nanouk, Rocket and Blizzid

Avalanches can reach speeds of over 100 kph (62 mph) within five seconds of fracture. That's potentially hundreds of thousands of tonnes. Imagine 20 football fields of snow piled three metres (nearly 10 feet) high, travelling at great speed consuming everything in its path.

Once it settles there is a critical window of only 15 to 20 minutes within which to rescue someone alive, after that their chances of survival decrease rapidly as each minute passes. Time is not on your side if you're buried in an avalanche.

First responders have to be mission-ready and deployable at a moment's notice. They often need to be heli-vacced directly to a location where they are expected to search large areas of snow with precision and great speed. And, once a subject is located, rescuers need to dig them out fast, something which is much easier to with four paws!

Speed, reliability, aptitude for accurately detecting humans buried under snow and the ability to start digging them out are all traits of highly trained avalanche rescue dogs.

Nanouk, Rocket and Blizzid are three fantastic dogs, from opposite ends of the globe, who are all trained in avalanche (snow) rescue.

Not all snow-buried people are victims of an avalanche. They may be people who have fallen ill and succumb to hyperthermia; elderly or very young people who have become lost or have fallen; or adventurers who have ignored safety warnings.

Matt Gunn, trainer and human partner to Blizzid and Rocket, confirms this when he notes it's often not the back-country skiers who are most at risk, as they are well prepared, but rather people who push their personal and the ski field's boundaries because they don't always know what they're doing and may be completely unprepared for an emergency.

No matter the reason, one thing people lost in snow have in common is once buried in a snowfall they are no longer visible and need rescuing urgently. This is where dogs like Nanouk, Rocket and Blizzid play a huge role.

Nanouk, or Nuki for short, is a five-year-old white Swiss shepherd and is dual-trained in avalanche and mountain rescue.

The Swiss were the first to acknowledge that, at best, avalanche and snow rescues were chaotic events. In the 1930s they developed a programme to train avalanche rescue dogs. Since then many countries have followed suit, realising the huge benefit in having dogs on the teams when rescuing and recovering buried victims. One dog can do the work of 20 people in less than an eighth of the time – which is pretty impressive and essential to rescues.

Statistically, during a search 20 humans can cover at best around 10 per cent of what a dog can during a fine search (where the search grids are close together) and at worst only 2.5 per cent during a hasty search. For example, an avalanche dog can search one hectare (2.5 acres) in approximately 30 minutes. The same area would take 20 people four hours using probe poles, and during a fine search the dog would take one to two hours to cover what would take humans 20 hours.

When your life is on the line and time is of the essence, there's no doubt about it – you want a dog searching for you. You want to hear the pacing and scruffing on the ground above, the deep inhalations and loud determined barking. In those circumstances, seeing a paw break through the ice, claw through a wave, or slip between some concrete has got to be a one of the best and most reassuring sights you will ever see.

In one incident, a cross-trained SAR dog became a little carried away and bit a subject when she found him. The man reported it was the best bite he'd ever had. He was happy to receive it and knew it was a sign that not only had he been found but he was still alive.

Training for an avalanche rescue dog is intensive, but dogs like Rocket and Blizzid love it. Rocket is the younger of the two

Retired now after ten years of service, Blizzid still loves the mountain.

dogs and Blizzid is now a retired avalanche rescue dog. They are both part of Matt's family. And as soon as Matt's truck hits the steep mountain access road Rocket starts letting the whole world know he's coming – as some collies are wont to do.

Blizzid, retired after 10 years' service, is far more refined and simply enjoys the ride up the mountain. A bigger thrill for her these days is stopping to smell the roses on the lakeside walks she takes with her human grandpa.

During their training and careers as operational avalanche rescue dogs, Nanouk, Blizzid and Rocket will be suspended under helicopters, towed in toboggans, have to ride on the shoulders of their handlers or endure any form of transport which delivers them to the scene in the fastest time. Some dogs would be terrified at the thought of their four paws leaving the ground, but not Nanouk – she loves her job so much that once, much to the amusement of seated human passengers, she tried to board a helicopter that wasn't there for her!

Rocket and his best human buddy Matt relax after a day's training.

Nanouk is off after receiving the word from Kitty to go find.

These dogs are trained in human scent detection and have the benefit of working in the snow. Snow is very porous, which means scent can travel through it easily and the cold preserves the scent's integrity. This makes working conditions easier than wilderness scenes, where the environment can be contaminated with the smell of other humans, other animals or food litter and so on.

Operational dogs on deployment after an avalanche use all their skills to locate the source of human scent. There are two possible sources of the scent – an item lost by the subject, which is identified as only an item and the dog keeps searching, or the actual subject, in which case the dog starts barking loudly and digging.

To the trained eye it is clearly visible when a dog catches a scent. For example, some dogs have a working tail, which is somewhat like a metronome moving high and with precise

Once a victim is located, the dog digs down until it either reaches the person or its human partners take over.

timing to the beat of their searching. Once they pick up a scent the tail will stop erect as the dog focuses in and follows the smell.

For other dogs, an indication of finding something may be as subtle as a head tilt or an ear swivel. This body language is a game changer and potential life-saver, so having a great relationship between dog and handler is paramount; the human partner must be able to read even the subtlest changes in their dog. They literally need to know their dog's every move. As both Matt Gunn and Kitty Gilli (the handler and life companion of Nanouk) will attest, it takes years to know your dog that well and it's certainly something most 'pet owners' never do.

Top

Matt rewards Rocket for all his hard work with a good game of tug.

Right

Millie also enjoys a game of tug, even after several years on the job.

Nanouk and Kitty work in Switzerland and have been called out on almost 20 occasions while working the mountains over winter and summer. Sadly, their job has mostly been to recover people post-avalanche. In fact, such is the nature of avalanches, over the past decade there has only been one occasion when a dog on their team has found a person still alive, but as Kitty says: 'They [the dogs] always find all missing people. And that is incredibly important for the grieving process of victims' families.'

71

Off duty, Nanouk still likes to enjoy the great outdoors.

It doesn't matter to Nanouk if the person is alive or not, she proceeds as trained at every deployment. Once the source of the scent is located she digs, and digs, until the rest of the team have arrived and relieve her. While dogs have been reported to have located an avalanche victim up to 12 metres (39 feet) under the snow, these incidents are rare. Most victims are located between two and four metres (6.5 and 13 feet) down. It can take dogs like Nanouk and Rocket half an hour to dig through two metres of packed snow.

In training, a person (often the dog's handler) is placed in a snow cave two metres (6.5 feet) down, at least half an hour before a search begins (with oxygen). A snowmobile is used to smooth out any visible hints before the dog arrives. This is challenging work not just for the dog but also for the handlers and volunteers who are buried during training. Not for the faint-hearted or the claustrophobic.

Once they are successful at finding a subject, the dogs are rewarded with play and they love it. Rolling around, joyously throwing their limbs about, belly up, torso swishing from side to side, with just as much enthusiasm and joy on snow as they show on grass or at the beach. Dogs love snow. One reason the cold has far less of an effect on them than their human counterparts is because dogs have a great heat exchange system.

'Dogs exchange heat at the end of their legs. Arterial blood flows to the end of their legs and then heats up venous blood before returning it to the heart,' Japanese scientist Hiroyoshi Ninomiya, an expert in animal anatomy from Yamazaki Gakuen University in Tokyo, explained in a study on the matter. 'In other words, they have a heat exchange system in their feet.'

Down off the mountain and off-duty, Blizzid and Rocket are spoiled with salmon – smoked or fresh, they're not fussy. It's one of the perks of living in the beautiful South Island of New Zealand. Matt recalls one incident when Blizzid was up on the table helping herself to a freshly smoked salmon, and upon being busted she simply continued eating it until she'd finished and then jumped down.

On the other side of the world, Nanouk resisted a meat platter for two hours before finally deciding she deserved a little self-reward for all her hard work and dedication. And while tuggy is the game of choice at work, Nanouk likes playing with plastic bottles filled with treats when she is off the clock. Snuggling in front of the fire watching TV and eating dried oxtail are also pretty awesome pastimes.

LandSAR dogs

Gemma and Odin

Imagine this . . . night falls; you didn't bring a jacket because the day had started out so bright and sunny. There is no cellphone reception. Looking around, everything seems the same. Somehow during the afternoon you've become disorientated as you enjoyed the peace and quiet that Nature had to offer. All you can see now are trees, the fading sky a distant backdrop. No hint of a landmark or a clue as to the direction in which your car is parked. The evening drizzle isn't cold yet, but after a few hours of being wet it will feel unbearable and all the noises of the wilderness will seem amplified as wildlife gets about its business in the dark. There's a sinking feeling creeping over you. Do you keep going or do you find a spot to wait out the night? What are the chances someone will find you?

Situations like this are very real and very serious. That's why dogs like Gemma and Odin are vital members of search and rescue teams.

Gemma is an incredible and talented three-and-a-half-year-old German shepherd who, since becoming operational at age two, already has a long list of deployments under her name as part of a LandSAR (Search and Rescue) team.

The official definition of the role of a SAR dog team is: to search for a person, or persons, who may be lost or buried and thought to be, or is, in distress or imminent danger. However, the actual role isn't as easy as it sounds.

Come rain, hail, snow, searing heat – these volunteer rescue teams often train long and hard. After a difficult day at the office, they can be out for days sleeping rough on the job, having to rappel down mountainsides, traverse deep crevices, cut their way through dense jungle or forest, leave their families and friends to find ours – and they don't get paid a cent. They are incredible, selfless people working with amazing dogs.

Gemma was adopted by Graeme Hill as a seven-and-a-half-week-old cute and mischievous puppy, specifically with the idea of training her for search and rescue work. She certainly rose to the challenge – but not before presenting her family with a few challenges of her own . . .

Gemma always loved the outdoors, the garden in particular, and clearly had her own ideas of how it should be designed. As a young pup she was able to communicate her ideas very clearly by, for example, digging up the freshly sewn vegetable garden. Gemma also developed a talent for standing on her hind legs to pluck lemons from the tree. Gin and tonic anyone?

When she was a young pup, Gemma loved helping with the laundry and would parade Mrs Hill's bra around the garden with great glee . . . obviously helping it dry.

These days with a new buddy to play with called Odin, Gemma has someone of her own kind to 'annoy'. This makes the dragway her family laid for her – namely the flowerbeds – much more fun to play in! Graeme is adamant that Gemma usually

Emerging after a long assessment weekend, Graeme and Gemma watch Odin jump for joy after qualifying as officially operational.

starts it, as she's pretty good at sparking Odin off by tapping him on his back with her paws until he chases her.

Odin is a three-year-old German shepherd Graeme adopted from the police force and successfully trained to be an operational SAR dog. Odin slotted right into the family, as he also loves gardening.

A dog's natural ability aside, the training for search and rescue work is time-consuming and arduous and must be constantly maintained, as the dogs have annual re-certification assessments. Graeme says: 'We want to keep them on top of their game, but we are very careful to always go back to the basics and make sure we always keep it fun for the dogs.'

In training the dogs are being taught from a very young age

to identify a human scent and, in the case of airborne human scent, follow it to its source. When tracking a person, they may either identify the track from the person's last known position, which could be the entry point to the area, or from an article belonging to the missing person, such as a piece of clothing which has been located by a team member.

Once on location during a SAR operation, there are two jobs the team can be charged with – one is an area search and the other is a tracking search.

An area search is when the dog team is asked to either confirm or eliminate the presence of a human within a delineated area so the wider SAR team can either proceed to search that area or move to a new location. Given their speed, agility and the accuracy of how they work in this manner, dogs can save lives and preserve human resources by cutting down the time it would take humans to do the same job by hours, if not days.

The dogs are also brilliant team members because they can do things humans cannot.

Says Graeme, 'It's not always about who locates the missing or lost – every member of the team plays an important role in the search operation whether in the field or at base, and a major part of that, which a dog team can provide, is eliminating areas to search or decision points at track junctions which may indicate which way someone walked. A good dog team can often do that quickly and thoroughly and cover very large areas and is best when combined with visual searchers. There are a range of factors which come into play as to how well this can be achieved, such as weather conditions, age of track, terrain etc. During a search Gemma can also assist by locating clues, which may be items with human scent such as a hat or glove, confirming a person's direction of travel at decision points, or indicating on recent human scent on the ground or a bush, for example – confirming someone had or had not been there recently.'

During an *area search* the dog will be off-lead, mostly air scenting (nose in the air), working at a fast pace, often out of sight of its handler but still working hard to locate human scent. Should this happen, the dog will work the scent 'cone' to its source, the lost person, and do one of two things, stay and bark to indicate the location to their human counterparts, or return to their handler, indicate and then guide them back to the subject. The latter being called a 're-find'. If they don't find evidence of human activity their handler will report back to SAR base a probability of detection for that area. Again, this will depend on the terrain and conditions. For example clearing a fenced tennis court would provide a 100 per cent probability no one is there.

When *tracking* a missing person or persons, the dog works in a slower, more methodical, paced manner, and is tethered to its handler via a long lead connected to the tracking harness it wears. It follows the line of scent, its nose constantly on the ground tracking a trail made up of human scent as well as various odours emitted from the ground disturbance created when a person walks. In the bush this can be crushed and decaying vegetation from footsteps and body contact with foliage.

Human scent is made up from the tens of thousands of skin cells, which are shed every minute; or evaporated perspiration; or respiratory gases; or decomposed gases by bacterial action on human skin or tissues; or the change in pheromones emitted with an emotional change in the person or group.

However, the line of scent decays over time if the person is still moving, and it can be contaminated by other people involved in the rescue or members of the public, which is why it is critical to get the dogs on the job as soon as possible.

For experts such as Gemma, that's just another challenge to overcome in the game. One night, around 9.30pm, Graeme and Gemma received a call for assistance from the police. A woman was missing. Friends had searched the immediate area while daylight remained, so getting through the contamination at the start, where her car had been found, was a bit tricky, but thankfully Gemma was able to overcome the challenge

Graeme knows how important play is to Gemma.

and within an hour had located the by now very cold woman. Although her condition was deteriorating fast, she was reaching out to pet Gemma. The young woman was taken to hospital and survived.

Most jobs are not as quick and, depending on the terrain, weather, situation and location, the dogs usually work for around two hours then take a break. Although many handlers report their dogs are so committed they don't want to stop and may search for days to find the subject. Should they be out overnight, these volunteer teams must be self-sufficient out in the wilderness.

When the search is over and it's time to return to safety, there is another advantage to having a dog on the team. The dog can often lead everyone out of the woods, so to speak, any time night or day by 'back tracking'. This not only means a more efficient exit, it also allows the human rescuers to concentrate on assisting the subjects who may be injured or to offer first aid to them without having to worry about navigating the way out. (Back tracking is also a technique used by police after arresting a subject to confirm their presence at a crime scene.)

'The great thing about Gemma,' says Graeme, 'is that once we have found people, especially at night during training or in a real situation, she has been really good at back tracking to our start point, and, if we are in the bush, we can then follow her out using her glow collar, which can make it easier than trying to navigate back out when we have people we are trying to assist as well.'

After a long search for a missing family of four who had become lost on a bush walk and taken refuge on a large fallen tree on rocks in the middle of a stream, Gemma proceeded to go one step further beyond the official call of duty, and lay down to comfort and sleep with the scared young children whilst they waited for other LandSAR teams to come and help evacuate the family out of the bush. Not surprisingly, when reunited several weeks after the incident the children said they loved Gemma!

So what do the dogs get out of all this hard work, aside from the joy of using their natural abilities to succeed at what is essentially a game to them? They get to play tug and they're a little bit spoilt when they get home.

For Gemma and Odin (who basically just likes what Gemma likes) that means dried pigs ears, greenies (dog chews) and a swim in the river chasing sticks or just relaxing on the deck in the sun.

Not that there hasn't been the odd occasion when Odin has self-rewarded, jumping on the picnic table, landing right on the sought after pizza, grabbing himself a slice then making a run for it! Running, probably, to his favourite spot – the large fishpond, where his joyful prancing isn't so much fun for the resident fish.

While Odin is new to this work, he qualified quickly. After

Opposite
Graeme and Odin being winched down to a remote location.

only two years on the job, Gemma already has a list of jobs to her name of which any rescuer would be proud. Gemma and Graeme have been either called out or put on standby on 34 occasions for searches and they have helped rescue a total of 13 people missing or lost, including three occasions where Gemma tracked right to the missing or lost parties – unfortunately one of whom was deceased. Graeme is adamant that it's always a team effort, with Gemma making a very valuable contribution to the team. As well, the team also includes people who have helped with training advice along the way.

It would be remiss not to take a moment to remember one of the world's oldest known search and rescue dogs, the Saint Bernard. Not the Saint Bernard we know today, which are the subject of much debate as to whether or not they are cross-breeds of the original or different dogs altogether – I'm referring here to the original dogs of the St Bernard Pass, which crosses the Alps between Italy and Switzerland. These famous dogs had short reddish brown and white coats and longer tails. As far back as 1660, and without any record of specialised training, the local monks' dogs acted as SAR, avalanche rescue, and hot-water bottles. They were companions as well as guard dogs, and even escorts for Napoleon's 250,000 troops, who successfully crossed the Pass over two decades, without a single loss. The famous barrels of brandy they carried around their necks may be just mythical, but not a bad idea, all the same.

Conservation dogs

Rocky and Jerry

'The word "ivory" rang in the air,
was whispered, was sighed. You would
think they were praying to it.'

Joseph Conrad, *Heart of Darkness*

Tanzania is home to what is estimated to be a quarter of the 75,000 elephants remaining in Africa today.

In October 2012, James Lembeli, chairman of the Tanzanian Parliament's Natural Resources Committee and a former National Parks official, offered his grim assessment of poaching. 'Thirty elephants per day. At the end of the year, you're talking about 10,000 elephants killed. Move around this country where you have populations of elephants: carcasses everywhere.'

Without serious action, there is the potential for elephants to become extinct within the next decade. According to the MIKE programme (Monitoring the Illegal Killing of Elephants), poachers are responsible for 60 to 90 per cent of elephant deaths in Tanzanian wildlife reserves.

Like many other African countries, Tanzania is losing its elephants because poverty, poor administration and corruption make ivory poaching an attractive money-making option. The outlook is exceptionally grim.

That's why some organisations and foundations aren't just standing by and waiting for international and local government action; they're taking it upon themselves to attempt to preserve these wonderful, majestic creatures, and are employing the natural skills of some very clever dogs to help. Rather ironic really, since elephants tend not to like dogs.

One such organisation is the Big Life Foundation in northern Tanzania. In conjunction with Canine Specialist Services International, they established the Kilimanjaro Dog Tracking unit in October 2011, with two dogs and four handlers selected from the local community. The dogs were trained to assist the Big Life anti-poaching community rangers in the Amboseli Kilimanjaro area, and to be available to assist anti-poaching scouts, the police and local communities.

The dogs charged with this very important duty are Rocky and Jerry.

Rocky is described as a very friendly, vocal and playful dog with a strong love of his work. He is considered the joker of the team and will do anything to try to convince people passing his run to engage in some play with him by jumping up and down and barking and begging. Joker though he may be off-duty, his favourite game is 'track that person' and when on duty he is incredibly focused and dedicated.

Jerry, the older of the two dogs, has a completely different temperament. He is silent and serious, more stealth-like in his work. Understanding (so to speak) the gravity of the consequences of his work, the team say Jerry approaches it very

Jerry and Rocky with their handlers Shinini, Lempris and Kalasinga.

earnestly, applying all his stamina and strength unreservedly to each event.

Events are the callouts which make their regular patrol work all the more challenging. The Big Life dog unit has had their skills put to use to identify poachers from a line-up days after a murdered elephant has been found, to track exactly which village the poachers have originated from, and, on occasion, also eliminated known poachers as suspects in a particular crime.

Richard Bonham writes on Big Life's website: 'Even if the poachers are not ambushed or stopped before the crime, they will almost definitely be caught with dogs after the crime. They cannot get away. Dogs can track from where poachers have killed up to one day past the event, and lead the team to the door of the poacher's house. This is a significant deterrent: the poacher knows nothing he can do will be able to change this. The Maasai in particular are terrified of tracker dogs, regarding them as somehow supernatural in their ability to track them down.'

And perhaps this is why ex-poachers, such as Mutinda, have changed sides and now work tirelessly to safeguard the endangered species they once sought to kill. Mutinda, having been taught by his father how to poach from age seven, knew no other life until he was approached by Big Life. He is now one of their 'ace dog handlers' and provides a wealth of knowledge and education to the team which can only come from someone who grew up on the land, watching the animals.

Because of the massive land area these dogs cover, sometimes getting from the kennels to the scene can take many hours, so the dog teams don't arrive until quite a while after the event, giving poachers more time to escape. However, even after time has elapsed usually the dogs will pick up a scent and track it to the nearest road or village or lead the rangers directly to the poachers.

In October 2012 Rocky and Jerry were called upon to help find poachers who had killed an elephant and stolen the ivory at Tarangire National Park. The dogs tracked from when they arrived in late afternoon until it was dark, their trail taking them through the park towards local villages.

After resting for the night the search team set off early the next morning with the strategy of visiting each village and asking the young men to line up so the dogs could check if any of them were the poachers.

A knife had been dropped by one of the poachers at the scene. It had been found and stored carefully to retain its scent. It was a great piece of evidence, as the handlers could bring it out regularly to refresh the dogs' noses.

After clearing one village they moved to the next. The dogs picked up the scent again, but it disappeared at the point at which the poachers had boarded a car and moved on. This was all good information. Narrowing in on the suspects, within half an hour of the last indication a vehicle was pulled over by police, and three men were then placed in a line-up. Sure enough, Rocky indicated on them immediately and wouldn't budge.

After the long track, taking place over several days, the dogs knew they had been successful and Rocky and Jerry received their much-anticipated prize, a good game of tug.

In another event, this time in January 2013, the dogs were

Jerry has his tracking gear put on.

called to assist at Lake Manyara National Park. Again an elephant poacher needed to be caught. Unfortunately, by the time the dogs arrived on the scene it had rained heavily and no track was immediately detectable. But before spirits could fall, a call came through from another team who had found a set of tracks (footprints), so the decision was made to track from those.

Rocky, who loves water, thought this job was the best. For six hours he led the team of rangers through marshes, pools of water and swamps to end up at a small village. Upon reaching a clear road the team changed dogs.

87

Rocky on the job, tracking elephant poachers.

Emmanuel, who was handling Jerry that day, had preserved the scent of the footprints found at the park on a piece of gauze. He opened the ziplok bag containing the gauze for Jerry and there was no restraining him. After a quick sniff to detect the scent, Jerry charged off, pulling Emmanuel behind him, and took them straight to a poacher's house.

Police forced entry into the house and discovered a huge pile of illegal fishing nets. So while the boys hadn't managed to find the elephant poacher, they caught someone poaching another species, who was later arrested.

For conservationists and animal lovers alike, the work these

88

dogs are doing is critical to the preservation of a highly endangered species. And it's a huge challenge as the area they need to cover is immense, covering thousands of square kilometres.

Originally their patrol area covered the Enduimet Wildlife Management Area, Kilimanjaro Conservancy and Kilimanjaro National Park. But, having established such a good reputation and with a growing understanding and appreciation of the benefits and skills of tracking dogs, they are now also called out to Lake Manyara and Tarangire National Parks and to Ngorongoro Conservation Authority.

The success of Rocky, Jerry and their human handlers is so well recognised that there are now plans in place to establish further, much-needed kennels.

Tanzania's current Director of Wildlife visited the dog unit in March 2013 and indicated that the Serengeti National Park and other areas also need the support of dogs. The ideal scenario is that one day these dogs will track down poachers before an animal is killed – and what a great day that will be.

Scat dogs

The work of conservation dogs isn't limited to just tracking humans. Dogs are also assisting in the conservation of other endangered species by tracking their scat.

Scat is really just a fancy name for poop, and poop is the not-so-fancy keeper of all sorts of critical information about a species – its diet, fertility, territorial range, gender and current levels of stress. Collecting scat is a non-invasive means by which scientists and conservationists can gather critical information about a species.

Easier said than done, however, for humans researching marine mammals.

Whale scat, although copious, brightly coloured (even neon in some cases) and strongly scented – even to the human olfactory sense – only floats for 30–60 minutes before it dissipates and sinks. Therefore, in a vast ocean area the chances of gathering a sample in time are slim. Humans were generally relying on their eyes to sight the scat, which was proving not very efficient or expedient, with a daily sample collection rate of one to none.

For such an incredibly endangered species as the North Atlantic right whale, the scat collection business was going far too slowly for scientists to gather the information needed to try to save these precious whales.

As the whale population began crashing, with only one calf being born in 2000, the situation was grave and the need for faster sample collection great. That was when Roz Rolland from the New England Aquarium in Boston came up with the idea of investigating enlisting the help of those with an awesome ability to smell . . . Bring in the dogs! As hoped, the introduction of scat-scenting dogs increased the sample collection fourfold.

The scat-scent trained dogs could smell the fresh poop, even just a smattering, at well over a kilometre (0.6 of a mile) away, on the water, with six-metre (20-foot) tides and variable wind speeds and directions. That's pretty awesome. The dogs would then indicate, using body language, which direction the captain should take the boat to reach the poop.

'Each dog has a unique change in behaviour that is consistent whenever it smells a specific odour,' says Barbara Davenport, the dogs' trainer 'By looking for those changes in ear set, tail movement, breathing rate, and facial expression, as well as taking into account tide and wind direction, researchers were able to figure out where to go. The dogs really are impressive. They know their business.'

Two very famous North Atlantic right whale scat dogs, Fargo, a three-year-old rottweiler, and Bob, a four-year-old beauceron mix, along with another famous orca-scat scenting dog Tucker, have quirks which make their drive to perform their jobs even more special. Fargo suffers from seasickness, Bob was terrified of the actual whales, and Tucker wouldn't swim and hated the water, but they loved their work and were happy to board the boat.

Samuel Wasser, director of The Center for Conservation Biology at the University of Washington in Seattle, hopes others will share his enthusiasm for the work the scat-scenting dogs carry out. 'The dogs are an incredibly valuable tool for gathering information. It's so much better than anything else I've seen out there by a long shot.'

But it's not just whale scat that dogs have been trained to detect. Scientists, conservationists and researchers studying wolves, kit foxes, grizzly bears, giant ant-eaters, Pacific pocket mice, moose, caribou, ring seals and even the elusive and highly endangered black-crested gibbon and Phayre's leaf monkey, in the remote mountaintops of Yunnan Province in China, all use dogs to help them find the important, information-rich droppings.

Search and rescue dogs and cancer detection dogs

Savannah

Negotiating the traffic on the streets and footpaths of a busy Bangkok thoroughfare requires special skills at the best of times. Amongst hawkers selling their wares, their babies sleep under the stalls, tourists mesmerised by the noise and the lights of the humming street life, there are people and traffic everywhere. Yet amongst all the chaos Savannah, Thailand's most highly qualified search and rescue dog, cruises along without fuss, sashaying her way through the crowds until she reaches the location she's looking for and veers to the right.

Tonight is not a work or training night for Savannah and her cohort Zambezi (see the chapter on pest control dogs); tonight is dinner out and a snow freeze ice-cream at a fast-food joint. Licking their treat straight from the cone to an amused crowd, Savannah helps herself first, then watches and appears to count every lick as Zambezi, the English setter, slowly takes her turn, savouring each lick until she almost bursts.

Like most working dogs, these girls know how to relax and play when off-duty, yet instantaneously shift gears into work mode the second it's required. Which is lucky – because like most search and rescue teams, these dogs and their handlers, are on call 24/7, 365 days a year.

Highly trained in multiple disciplines, both Savannah and Zambezi are shining examples of the versatility and capability of dogs.

Savannah has many strings to her working bow. This adorable, soft golden retriever is an operational search and rescue dog, certified under the International Rescue Dog Organization, and has been operational since 2009. She is cross-trained in mobility assistance, for which she is an ambassador in Thailand. Savannah's therapy work takes her to visit senior citizens and children. And, as if that doesn't keep her busy enough, Savannah is participating in a ground-breaking cancer detection research project – but more about that later.

Beautiful Zambezi, the younger of the two dogs, is also qualified for search and rescue work. She loves to snuggle up to strangers when on duty as a therapeutic visitation dog, and is Thailand's only qualified bed-bug detection dog.

That's a pretty big CV for one family!

Search and rescue

Savannah is qualified for both LandSAR and Urban Search and Rescue work. USAR teams around the world have the massive task of searching for people buried amongst the rubble of collapsed structures. This may be after a natural disaster, the collapse of a structure, mass transportation accidents or any number of man-made catastrophes.

Savannah and her loyal human, Sue Redmond, have been deployed on a number of SAR missions. Most notably, they were deployed to a building collapse in Nonthanburi, north of Bangkok, where Savannah located the body of a missing construction worker, giving closure to his family and allowing them to carry out their religious rituals. Savannah quickly found the man buried under 50 centimetres (20 inches) of solid concrete, yet it took 12 hours to remove the rubble before his body could be recovered.

In situations such as this, it is paramount to deliver dogs like Savannah and Zambezi to the location as fast as possible. These are the brave teams you see on the news, rushing into the scene of mass destruction to initiate their critical work just when everyone else is panicking and rushing to get out.

Because USAR dogs are trained to detect human scent, any living human scent (they are not scent-discriminating for a specific person, like a tracking dog), the less contaminated the area is by other rescue workers the better. And because, unlike avalanche rescue, there is still the possibility of finding someone alive

many hours and even days after an incident, the USAR dog teams sometimes have to work long deployments. Following the Christchurch earthquake, the dogs worked 32 hours straight (with medical and food breaks), and during tragedies such as the World Trade Center collapse in New York, 400 dog teams worked for weeks.

Proud to be part of the team, SAR dogs wear a tag of merit.

94

Savannah, Zambezi, Sue and Andy cross the river in the early morning to begin training.

Nothing fazes Savannah, not even the bustle of busy Bangkok streets.

Writing about the dogs deployed to the World Trade Center, 'Angel' an online writer for Environmental Graffiti described their role eloquently:

'What a dog could do with its nose was invaluable in the search. What a dog could do with its heart was equally invaluable. Handlers, cops, and firemen were under unbelievable stress at the former World Trade Center. These canine emergency workers were tremendously valuable for their therapeutic influences on their human counterparts at the disaster site. It was beyond

Sue prepares Savannah for work.

amazing what a licking tongue could do to lift a crushed human spirit, restoring morale to discouraged and depressed workers at Ground Zero.'

USAR dogs are exceptionally brave, working on, under and through structures which can be volatile – disappearing into voids, crawling on their bellies, squeezing through obstacles, going where humans can't and using their phenomenal scent-tracking abilities to seek out the exact location of those trapped beneath rubble, all to win their prize: a game of tug. In Savannah's case, tug would be with Mr Squirrel, her favourite.

These dogs work in an environment which is often dangerous and tremendously noisy, so much so that weather conditions aren't even a consideration. All that combined with smoke, fumes and dust, bright flood-lights, hysterical relatives, reporters, heavy machinery, fire, police and civil defence – all day and throughout the night they carry on with unbelievable focus and drive.

But dogs are not robots, they can and do become tired and they can also become disheartened and depressed when they are unsuccessful. USAR dogs are trained to find living people (unlike cadaver dogs), and when that turns into finding deceased people or body parts, in a massive disaster and a highly stressful environment, the dogs can reach breaking point. Recognising this, handlers will often set up scenarios on site and hide, allowing their dogs to have a successful find, boosting their drive and reviving their spirits.

Angel also wrote about the sad side of the job. 'One 12-year-old SAR dog found the bodies of two missing firemen. The dog curled in a ball next to them and wouldn't move. Even later on, the dog wouldn't eat. As if too heartbroken at the tragic loss of life, the dog lost its will to go on until his handler took him home. These dogs want, with all their hearts and all their training, to find people alive. There was so much death surrounding the SAR dogs, but they worked night and day, without complaining about hazards or their injuries; they kept working even when there was no hope left of finding a survivor.'

Wilma Melville, president and founder of the National Disaster Search Dog Foundation and part of a FEMA (Federal Emergency Management Agency) SAR unit in California, USA, explains: 'Wilderness searching is atmosphere-friendly to dogs. But in urban SAR, they're working in unnatural surroundings, amid rubble, pipes, "tippy" things.'

Keep in mind also that many of the dog teams, like Savannah and Sue and Zambezi and Andy, are volunteers. They train year-round during the week, in weekends, over holidays, in soaring heat and torrential rain. The climate is uninviting to volunteers and unsavoury to most dogs at the best of times. During training, the hiding victims not only put up with all weather conditions and dirt and dust, bumps and bruises and long hours of being crammed into a tiny space, in some countries they must also be wary of poisonous snakes and killer spiders.

For anyone, being buried beneath thousands of tons of concrete and metal rubble is terrifying. It's not only the shock of the massive catastrophe which just consumed you, it's the dark, it's the pain, it's the fear of not knowing where you are or how long you may be there, it's not being able to move and not knowing how long your air will last. When you're in this horrific situation there are no words to describe how it feels to hear a dog somewhere close by barking loudly.

With their phenomenal sense of smell, dogs prove better than technology at locating buried humans. This is because dogs have an average of 220 million scent receptors to our mere five million and they use 10 per cent of their brain to process scents whereas humans only use 0.29 per cent. In layman's terms, a dog can smell one rotten apple within two billion barrels of apples, or a teaspoon of sugar diluted in 4.5 million litres (a million gallons) of water – the equivalent of two Olympic swimming pools.

Cancer detection

For medical practitioners and patients suffering from an illness such as cancer, bio-detection dogs may be a dream come true.

While still in its formative stages, since 2004 dogs have been in training to detect cancer from either breath or urine samples from patients. Trials have taken place in the USA, England, Japan, Germany and now Thailand, screening for recognition of lung, bladder, breast, prostate, melanoma, colorectal and liver cancers.

But how can they do this? Studies suggest dogs can detect the tiny amounts of chemicals called alkanes and benzene derivatives which are not present in healthy tissue but may be exuded from malignant tumours. Essentially, the dogs are spotting the difference when a body odour changes. Given their ability to detect a scent at parts per trillion, it isn't a stretch to understand how they may be able to detect these subtle changes in human odour.

Dogs such as Savannah participate in double-blind studies. This is when neither the dog nor their handler knows which sample contains breath or faeces from a person with cancer – and which do not. The samples are in vials, which are put on a carousel and then spun around to avoid anyone inadvertently making suggestions to the dogs as to which vials are which. The dog is brought in and walks around the carousel from one vial to another, and will sit and indicate the one they think has the scent of cancer. Some trials have reported up to 90 per cent accuracy.

It's important to note the dogs are differentiating between scents and indicating which one isn't like the others; they are not diagnosing cancer *per se*.

Although still in the very early stages of research, it's trailblazing work, which could have a huge impact should results prove dogs to be as accurate as they have been during trials to date. Scientists and technicians around the world have been trying, unsuccessfully, to develop an artificial nose to compete with or at least have a similar ability to a dog's. It has to be said: you can't beat Nature!

Explosive detection dogs

Drake, Bruce, Roc and Nitro

For the majority of the world's population, explosive detection dogs (EDDs) are never seen, never thought about and certainly under-appreciated. Explosive detection dogs are the brave scouts who go in first to either 'clear' an area of any suspected explosive device or material, or locate it so the explosive ordinance disposal (EOD) specialists can disarm and/or remove it before it can cause anybody any harm.

A Vietnam War veteran once said: 'They are the only weapon system we ever devised to save lives.'

These dogs work wherever they are needed – in buildings, stadiums, hotels, planes, ships, deserts, jungles, at large public gatherings and on battlefields all over the world. Many EDD teams work in stealth – they come in, do their job and get out without anyone ever knowing they were there. That's one side of their job.

The other side is to have a strong public presence, working 'front of house'. Interestingly, the Israeli Police discovered that having the dogs working 'out the front' rather than behind the scenes at ports of departure such as airports acted as a stronger deterrent to any potential criminal activity or terrorism.

It has to be the most dangerous job in the world for a dog. Yet for dogs like Bruce, Roc, Nitro and, across the world in Afghanistan, Drake, it's all a big fun game of hide-and-seek and find-and-get to play. But the reality is, at times these handlers and dogs work under very dangerous conditions.

Bruce and his canine pals are shiny-coated, clearly loved and well-cared-for friendly dogs who love to play. If you saw them on the street you would never guess these boys are employed in such serious work, but if you see them in action you know they are more than fit for purpose – and they love their work!

Bruce, Roc, Nitro and Drake could be called highly trained, but that would suggest their training days were over, whereas for these dogs training lasts until retirement. To remain at the top of their game, ahead of their adversaries and to keep their skills sharp, handlers and canines train on a daily basis. The world of explosives is ever-moving and these boys, and other dogs just like them, have to stay one step ahead of those whose intention is to harm and kill.

For EDDs, their training consists of identifying a number of ingredients used individually or in composite to make explosive devices, along with detonation cords, igniters, time fuses and blasting caps. They work with only one handler and that handler has to be re-certified annually to work with the one specific dog. Knowing and trusting each other intimately is essential, because their work is so intensive. Like other handlers already mentioned, they must recognise the most subtle of alerts in their dog, a twitch of the ear, a slight stiffening of the tail, a small shake. Each dog is an individual and so works differently from another.

Unlike other detection dogs, which must be very vocal and sometimes physical with their alerts, EDDs are passive and still when they locate a potential explosive. Any overt movement could cause a detonation. Once they have signalled a device, they are recalled to safety and their handlers will clear, cordon and contain the area so the EOD team can take over.

Brett Clarke, handler of Bruce, says it's very clear when Bruce is having a 'perve', his tail goes around and around, but if he's on scent it's stiff and straight.

In a rare interview with *60 Minutes*, Green Beret, Sergeant First Class Chris Corbin with the Seventh Special Forces Group discussed his dog Ax, a Belgian malinois EDD, with whom he worked in Afghanistan. During their last tour together, SFC Corbin wasn't paying attention to his dogs as intently as usual and failed to recognise Ax's signal and learnt the hard way.

The day had been going well. Ax had already discovered one bomb and the team moved to a new location which had already been cleared. SFC Corbin noticed Ax had started pulling down on his lead instead of forward, and thought he must have passed a dog or had something on his shoe and as a result wasn't walking properly. With a flash of recognition that came just a second too late, SFC Corbin saw wires coming from a building, knew they were in an area full of explosives, and the intense attention Ax was paying to his foot was because he was standing on one. While Ax wasn't hurt in the explosion, SFC Corbin lost both his lower legs.

In some cases, such as with military working dogs who are deployed on longer tours than their human counterparts, they may be handed over to another handler when theirs finishes a tour of duty. In such cases, the dog is still only under command of that new soldier, and many retire with their handler or handler's family at the end of their active career.

Bruce, like Roc and Nitro, is an explosive detection dog who is also called upon to assist other government agencies, should the need arise. His job is to deter criminal activity, clear hangers, cargo holds, baggage, search vehicles and much more, which he does at great speed and with unbelievable efficiency. These dogs work at a constant 97 per cent. As an example, it would only take around five minutes for two dogs to clear an empty 747 cargo hold – something it would not only take humans much longer to do, even with the assistance of technology, but it would also be almost impossible for them to access some if the areas a dog can scent.

Bruce takes a break from training.

Bruce is a five-year-old border collie huntaway cross, who has been with Brett since he was 10 weeks old. He's described as a very loyal dog – so loyal, that if Brett is on the couch watching a bit of TV on a day off, Bruce will flick the window latch with his nose and launch himself through the window onto him, just to see if he needs anything. Or to see if there may be a tennis ball handy, his favourite off-duty toy, especially when it's thrown at the park.

There is no breed of dog better for this job than any other – rather it's the skills of the individual dog that count. They must be 'high drive' and have a 'good nose', something which can be found in both young puppies and mature dogs. Oh, and they also have to be medium-sized so they can fit into places which need to be searched, as well as stand on chairs and sniff up into overhead lockers.

Roc, like most of the dogs on his team, was a pound dog. Full of kennel cough and emaciated, among numerous other complaints when he was dumped there, his handler Andrew Wells and his boss Don McKenzie, saw something special in this boy. They pulled him from the pound even though he was so sick and gave him an assessment, which he passed with flying colours. Roc never returned to the pound. The team knew that if he was responding so well when he was so sick, imagine what he would do when he was well. Roc was returned to full health and he is now 'an awesome dog'.

Globally military, private security firms and large organisations such as the United Nations employ EDDs to assist in combat explosive detection and mine sweeping (clearing) and humanitarian de-mining missions. Most of their work remains highly classified.

Combat explosive detection is when a dog is deployed to work with their handler in a 'theatre' (war zone). Here the dog's job is reconnaissance work to detect and indicate the presence of a mine, improvised explosive device (IED) or explosive material in an unsecured or unknown area, vehicle or on a person. This is

Roc with his best dog buddy on and off duty, Nitro.

a much simplified explanation of the extremely dangerous and fraught work these dog teams do to protect their fellow soldiers and civilians alike.

Roc is rewarded for good work by a happy Andrew.

SFC Corbin attributes the success of military working dogs to the fact they think they're invincible, partly because they never know they are in danger and partly because they're not trained to fail.

Humanitarian work for dog teams requires them to assist other de-mining professionals in clearing minefields post-conflict so locals can safely go back to using the land. Restoring life and a sense of normality to families who have been living with the constant threat of explosions, injury and death is their reward for doing this intense and imminently dangerous work.

According to The International Committee of the Red Cross, more than 800 people are killed and 1200 maimed by landmines every single month – most of them children, women, and the elderly.

In places like Bosnia and Zimbabwe, landmines were buried in their millions, some even dropped randomly and *en masse* from helicopters and planes. Post-conflict it is taking years to decommission all these explosive devices. The teams can only work safely in areas of 10 square metres (100 square feet) at a time to avoid triggering tripwires, and the mines were planted in areas that are as large as 32,000 square kilometres (12,000 square miles).

The speed and accuracy with which the dogs work must be acknowledged as having helped accelerate this land reclamation process. Two dogs working in shifts can do the work of 20 men. And safety-wise the dogs are able to go either under or over tripwires, which are usually placed at human shin or chest height.

Out in the field, metal detectors, mine sweepers, prodders and even hand-held high-tech state-of-the-art detectors have all been supplanted by the nose of a dog. This is the reason why researchers in Europe and the USA are furiously working away, so far unsuccessfully, to replicate what Mother Nature created, so they can put it in a machine.

In October 2012, *The New York Times* quoted Dr Paul Waggoner, senior scientist at the canine detection research institute at Auburn University, as saying: 'We really are not going to ever be able to surpass the dog in terms of its general ability as a mobile sensing platform. [And] over the years "the instrument guys" have come to appreciate dogs even more.'

The same article quotes Aimee Rose of explosion detector company Flir as confirming what most readers of this book already know . . . 'Dogs are awesome. They have by far the most developed ability to detect concealed threats.'

Ex-Navy Seal Mike Ritland simplifies the phenomenal scent discrimination and detection abilities of a dog by using the example of beef stew. He says most people know dogs can smell better than humans. What they don't know is that, where a human will walk into a room and smell beef stew, a dog will smell potatoes, carrots, beef, flour, celery, water, salt and so on. And not just smell but be able to identify each and every ingredient. 'You can't hide anything from them. It won't work because you can't fool a dog's nose.'

Retired Lieutenant Colonel George Hulse of Australia says: 'People underestimate the role of dogs in the military and corrective services. Sometimes these dogs do things they were never trained for. They'll find people and non-explosive devices – they'll find machine guns hidden in walls, concreted in the ground. It's incredible how they find these things, and we're still, after all these years, not sure how they do it but we're very glad that they do.'

Although these dogs have the natural ability to excel in this job, it would be remiss to not to acknowledge that in their selfless ability to work for man, to save lives dogs sometimes suffer. They give their health and sometimes their lives. Mine detection dogs and their handlers are usually the first to go into a potentially dangerous area.

US Army Sgt Garrett Grenier, a dog handler with the 49th Engineer Detachment (mine dogs) explains their work to Sgt Christopher Bonebrake in his article 'A dog's life: mine dogs train to save lives', published on the US Army website:

> On a typical mission we primarily support route clearance. We dismount when needed and clear the route ahead of the convoy or patrol. The process of clearing a minefield is a long and arduous one. A simple mistake could send both dog and handler to the hospital or worse. Therefore the handler must ensure the dog stays close and walks a straight line through a danger-area.

Garrett keeps his dog on a leash to facilitate this and controls him with short sharp commands. When the dog finds the 'mine' he alerts and, if correct, is rewarded with his favourite toy and lots of attention.

'Working in itself is fun to him [Drake],' said Garrett. 'It's kind of like a game.'

And when confronted with the accusation that this work isn't fair on the dogs because they don't know the danger they are in, SFC Corbin has one answer: 'I could make him scared of it, make him not do his job and send soldiers to the same death.'

It's distressing for the dog, their handler and a whole unit when anything happens to the dogs. Andrew tells of one incident where Roc got his paw caught between two moving baggage conveyor belts and it was all but torn off. Andrew recalls that it took only six minutes to get Roc to the 24-hour emergency surgery, a trip which would usually take much longer.

And watching Arko, Mike Ritland's semi-retired canine partner, happily running around his farm in Texas, you would

Drake is rewarded with play after a tough day in the field.

never know this was a dog who continued to maintain control of an enemy fighter even after being shot point-blank in the chest by the guy during the struggle.

As Mike says, 'It's hard to explain the physical capabilities of these dogs and hard to comprehend, even if you see it.' He was thankful that every single step he took when on deployment in 'hell on earth' was with Arko, knowing each step was far less likely to be his last with his dog at his side.

And, thankfully, unlike days of old, if there is any sign of

Sergeant Grenier and Drake heading back to base. It's all a game to Drake.

illness or worse, should a dog be wounded in the field, he is picked up and treated immediately and if necessary heli-vacced to hospital.

These dogs are high-value team members and in war-torn nations enemy forces have realised their incredible ability, making them the target of assassination attempts by putting bounties on their heads. A *60 Minutes* correspondent was told by a Taliban leader in Afghanistan that on their last mission they 'were instructed to open fire on the dogs first and deal with the soldier later.'

When asked about his dog, the one he hopes can retire with him, Sgt Grenier says:

> Drake is more than just a Military Working Dog to me. He is a friend, a buddy and a part of my family. We spend a lot of time around each other, especially while deployed, when we are constantly together. We hang out during the long hot days out on mission and at night back on base. We keep each other company while away from our family and friends back home. Drake and the other MWDs put a smile on the face of everyone we encounter over here, reminding them of their dogs back home. We trust each other with our lives and work together so we can both go home in one piece. Drake takes all the risk out in front of everyone else clearing the route ahead of us for IEDs that we would otherwise be unable to detect. He works hard to keep us safe and he has fun doing it. He doesn't ask for much in return, just some love and his favourite toy.

Customs and biosecurity dogs

Ralph, Shadow and Boss

If you've travelled or you watch reality television shows on border security, chances are you would have seen one or more of these, often very cute, dogs eagerly traversing baggage on the carousels or weaving their way around passengers, tails high and wagging, nose working at maximum capacity. Which for a dog like a beagle means having around 330 million scent receptors on the go – and that's a 100 million more than other dog breeds and 325 million more than humans.

What are they doing? They're looking for illegal narcotics, restricted goods or biohazard items such as food or other animals.

Around the world, in places like New Zealand, Australia, the UK and the USA, these detector dogs work tirelessly to patrol

A detection dog checks baggage on an airport carousel.

boarders at airports, seaports, international rail stations, cargo depots and international mail centres.

They are trained to detect things such as narcotics, tobacco, cash, firearms, animal-based products and fruit. These dogs often work in conjunction with other agencies such as the police and/or with technology such as X-ray machines to ensure that border searches are thorough.

The training and employment of dogs for detecting illegal substances began in the 1960s, and by the 1970s government agencies throughout the world were using detector dogs for various specialised tasks.

In narcotic detection, for example, dogs are trained to detect a wide variety of illegal drugs, and each successful find means fewer drugs on the streets. The dogs can detect illicit narcotics such as cocaine, heroin, MDMA (ecstasy), amphetamine, methamphetamine, cannabis and precursors used to manufacture crystal methamphetamine or 'P'.

Narcotic detector dogs (NDDs) in Australia have had to deal with some unusual challenges, with criminals trying to conceal narcotics in strange places. Their efforts are wasted as they're clearly unaware that a dog's nose cannot be fooled. People have tried and failed to traffic narcotics by trying to hide their drugs in things such as shampoo bottles, metal framing, tins of tomatoes, fake religious relics and jewellery, and also tried avoiding detection with impregnated fabric and clothing. Doesn't work. The dogs detect the lot. It is very important to note that these working dogs themselves never come into contact with the drugs they detect and never become addicted to them.

Renowned for their breeding and training programme, Australian Customs and Border Protection has provided assistance for a number of countries, including Malaysia, Guam, Samoa, Taiwan, Thailand, the USA and China. New Zealand has been instrumental in supplying dogs and training for countries such as Argentina, Korea, Canada and the American state of Hawaii.

The dogs employed in this job are friendly and unthreatening for a very good reason. It is important for these dogs to be very sociable with humans because they have to interact with hundreds of strange people every day and are not allowed to react negatively towards them. The UK Border Agency says about their dogs: 'Their unassuming, friendly nature allows them to quietly mingle among travellers without causing unnecessary annoyance.'

Happy in their work, their tails wag because their job, although extremely serious and important to national health and well-being, is an all-day-long game of hide-and-seek. And when they discover something they receive a reward: a game of tug or some food treats.

Cute and cheerful as they are, these dogs are of such high value to border security and have proven to be such a nemesis

A detection dog checks packages at an international mail centre.

to would-be criminals, one now has to work with his own body guards.

In October 2012, the *Daily Mail* reported that a drug gang in Rio de Janeiro had issued a death order against a brown Labrador named Boss, after the sniffer dog uncovered 300 kilograms (660 lb) of cannabis. Major Vitor Valle, from Rio's military police dog squad, said Boss will continue to work but will now be protected by nine policemen.

An Irish newspaper, the *Daily Edge*, reported online in June 2012 that cannabis resin with an estimated street value of €319,000 was seized by the Revenue's Customs Service at Rosslare, with a little help from its new sniffer dog, Ralph. While a foreign national was arrested during the operation, 53 kilograms (116 lb) of cannabis resin was seized when officers stopped and searched a car disembarking a ferry from France.

On 19 March 2013, in a report on ABC 7 News Chicago, investigators said 30 lb (14 kilograms) of opium were seized at the International Mail Facility near Chicago's O'Hare Airport. A US Customs detection dog named Shadow sniffed out the drugs, which were hidden in four separate shipments in the airport's mailroom.

The shipment came from Laos and was invoiced as dresses and traditional medicines. When Chicago Customs and Border Protection officers tested the dresses, woodchips, leaves and twigs, they found them saturated with opium.

The drugs have a reported street value of almost $500,000, according to Chicago Customs and Border Protection officials – and might have slipped through the cracks and landed on the streets if it weren't for the awesome nose of Shadow.

Pest control dogs

Zambezi

Fire ants

The South American red fire ant, which has spread around Australasia, poses a huge threat to the environment it invades.

'This notorious pest is capable of consuming a large quantity of food during its rapid propagation, devastating agricultural products, threatening the well-being of both livestock and humans, and seriously affecting the native animal species in the invaded areas.' (Adams 1986, Lofgren 1986, Allen et al. 1994).

In the arid heat of Northern Australia teams of detection dogs work hard at keeping the invading ants under control. South American red fire ants are highly toxic, so as well as rigorous detection training the dogs must undergo supervised veterinary-controlled tests to make sure any exposure to the ants or ant bites isn't going to send them into potentially fatal anaphylactic shock. The dogs can detect even a single ant or a new colony forming, giving conservationists plenty of time to react and eradicate the ants.

Their working environment can become extremely hot, so the dogs work shifts of 15 minutes at a time, for up to four hours per day. The dogs are closely monitored by their handlers for any signs of stress or distress in this 40°C workplace. This is necessary as some dogs have such a strong drive to work they don't want to stop and it's not medically safe for them to keep going.

Bed-bugs

Zambezi is a fully qualified bed-bug detective. She has such a good nose for the bugs that she could clear a hotel in one whiff, if the situation should arise.

Although dogs have an immense ability to smell, it isn't something which is always 'turned on' in dogs, as they aren't naturally drawn to or interested in many of the odours we want them to detect. Therefore, in order for humans to engage their natural ability to our advantage, dogs are trained to sniff out something we want in return for something they want – making it a win-win game. In Zambezi's case being rewarded for her work is an extra bonus, as she seems to take an exceptional delight in just finding the bugs themselves – although not as much excitement as she has when chasing cats.

Zambezi has a super snout.

Sue recalls one incident when Zambezi broke command and chased a cat way out of sight, nearly giving them a heart attack because

Zambezi cools down after some search-and-rescue training.

they live in such a busy city, only to be found later on the second floor of a car park looking very sheepish.

Training for 'nose' work is primarily the same whether it's for bed-bugs, narcotics, currency, truffles or scat. A very simplified explanation is that over a period of time the dog is initially taught to recognise a particular scent, then is rewarded for discriminating that scent amongst others, then for finding the scent at a distance or in an unknown location. Incremental steps are taken in training until eventually the dog is only rewarded when they discover the source of the scent in a generalised environment.

Properly trained dogs are excellent for bed-bug detection work, because they use their olfactory sense instead of their visual sense, which means they can locate the bugs not just in beds but in walls, crevices, furniture – basically anywhere they may be. Dogs have been known to detect as few as one single bed-bug or egg, and to discriminate between living and dead bugs, eggs, cast skins and faeces.

Because this is such a burgeoning field of work around the world, not just for businesses like hotels but also many private citizens wanting to know if their beds are safe at night – definitely not wanting the 'bed-bugs to bite' – there has been an explosion of dogs being advertised who have not been properly trained. They aren't second-rate dogs, rather under-qualified for the job. If you engage a bed-bug detection dog, like Zambezi, make sure he or she is certified by the appropriate ministry of health for your country or state.

And after all her work is done . . . Zambezi likes to curl up on the pillows to sleep, hiding her face but still wagging her tail if she knows you are there.

Bird strike

Bird strike is a serious threat to all aeroplane pilots. While few incidents end as dramatically as the US Airways flight 1549, which successfully ditched in the Hudson River in New York in 2009 after bird strike, the potential for mass casualties from a similar incident is ever-present.

Birds or deer on runways or around airports are pests and pose a critical threat to all travellers. One successful way of managing this threat has been to employ dogs to keep the birds away by chasing them off the land and preventing them from building nests or mating. Bird-chasing behaviour is something many dog owners will be familiar with, and many probably wish their dog could find fruitful paid employment doing what they enjoy.

The Birdstrike Control Program in the USA trained and placed the first dog to be employed by a commercial airport for bird strike control, as well as the first dogs to be used by the US Air Force, the Canadian Air Force, the Israeli Air Force and Canadian commercial airports. The Birdstrike Control Program was also

Chester and Piper, pest detection dogs in training, think they smell a rat or possum up a tree.

the first in the world to introduce a trained dog for bird control in the aquaculture industry.

In Australia, in July 2011, bird strike management experts Avisure became the first in the country to train a dog to watch over Gold Coast Airport, reported online by the *Daily Mail*.

Joe, the black Labrador, was rescued from death row at the pound where he was assessed as being unsuitable for a family pet. How ironic, then, that those same qualities which could have condemned Joe, made him a highly valued member of Avisure. Happily for Joe, he was rehabilitated and trained by Craig A Murray Dog Training to perform a very important role.

In the report, Joe's handler, Martin Ziviani says: 'I've been at the airport for five years, utilising all sorts of bird strike prevention techniques, and Joe's the latest tool.' He said Joe was trained to target birds posing a threat, then once the threat of birds was negated, return to his handler for a reward in the form of play. 'He's not a threat to birds and he's only trained to disperse them.'

On their website Craig A Murray say about Joe: 'The birds in the locations he works both revere him and fear him but he is truly an environmentalist and a humanitarian, all in all one happy fun-loving Labrador dog. His human partner, biologist Martin Ziviani, would not swap his canine work partner and he takes Joe home as his lifelong friend.'

Farm dogs

Herks

The sun rises, golden over the parched, tawny land. The rains are late this year and the cattle are hungry. The lingering smell of fire-brewed coffee fades as the old cowboy saddles up and whistles to his dogs.

There would be few people who haven't seen the prowess of farm dogs, whether in the movies, on television or in person, crossing paddocks, scaling hillsides, crouching, barking, riding on motorbikes or shadowing horses. Just the mention of the words 'working dogs' to people in countries such as New Zealand, Australia, South Africa, England and Argentina and the image of scruffy, scrawny tough mutts of no particular breed immediately spring to mind, either that or the long-haired, eyes hidden behind matted fringes traditional 'sheep' dogs.

The role these dogs play in the management of livestock like sheep, cattle, goats and reindeer is vital to farmers and stockmen. Most often there will be only a handful of dogs to muster hundreds of animals, finding any that stray as they keep herds and flocks together and out of danger.

Hercules was a spectacular example of a farm dog, and not just because of his stunning good looks, silky soft long coat or even his big heart. Born and raised on a South Island farm in New Zealand, Herks, Mr Perkins, Herkus Perkus or any one of the nicknames he responded to, was the progeny of good working parents, from whom he inherited an awesome work ethic. Many farmers claim good working farm dogs are bred and their abilities are a force of Nature.

In the introduction to his book *Pup Pen to Paddock*, Lloyd Smith surmises the role of farm dogs succinctly when comparing them to all the changes technology has brought to farming 'But one aspect of agriculture has remained constant: moving stock around our farms and stations, which can't be done satisfactorily without dogs.'

Once again, we find technology cannot replace or do the work of a dog. Certainly it can assist the work of dogs – helicopters transport dogs into the high country of large stations – and advanced research into feeding working dogs helps farmers keep their dogs healthier than ever before. Uncommonly for a pet dog and certainly a rarity amongst farm dogs, Herks' father Bill lived to the ripe old age of 20 – a testament to the care he received from his human parents, Joc and Stew Howden.

Modern methods of training and a better understanding of the nature of canines means the farmer–dog relationship has advanced from where it once started. Herks would surely attest to that as he sits in his manicured garden, enjoying the sun and some fresh paua and oysters after a long walk and a game of fetch. Retirement suits him, except if there are chickens around, then his prey drive kicks into full gear, which makes him very unpopular with the neighbours.

There are different categories of working farm dog – not to be confused with livestock guarding dogs. They can be a heading, huntaway, heeler, tending or handy dog.

The heading dog (sometimes called an eye dog) doesn't bark

Grand old Herks enjoys the breeze of retirement.

but rather out-stares or 'eyes' the other animal until it moves in a desired direction. They are also responsible for leading (stopping or holding up the stock until given the OK), then moving back (taking the pressure off) to allow the stock to continue. They really come into their own when crossing roads or if the farmer needs to redirect the flock or herd or if they approach a dangerous area.

In contrast, huntaway dogs are encouraged to bark, particularly on command, to move stock. Huntaways also have more physical contact with the stock. Jumping on the sheep's backs, they work with farmers in yards and will also use their body to push sheep if needs be, without harming them. Herks' father was a huntaway, but his mother enjoyed riding the backs of sheep. Herks likes to use his bark to ward off those evil things called cars and trucks.

A handy dog has the skills of both a heading dog and a huntaway, and can work with a farmer or cowboy as a multipurpose dog.

Heelers, as their name suggests, have a habit of nipping animals, particularly cattle, on the heels instead of barking – a trait which doesn't work so well with vehicles.

For large areas of unfenced land or potentially dangerous areas such as road crossings, tending dogs work as a 'living fence'. They patrol boundaries and guide stock to the correct location while preventing them from crossing over to unprotected land, or from eating valuable crops.

Tip, a New Zealand huntaway, negotiates terms with a stubborn steer.

One very hot summer's day 500 heifers broke into a winter feed crop. Herks almost worked himself to death after trying on his own (accompanied by Joc and Stew) to shift the stock back to where they were meant to be. He worked for hours, determined to complete his job and afterwards staggered and collapsed several times before Stew could reach him to carry him to the water race where he sat for some time, cooling down. One of the possible reasons dogs work to this extreme is because they have a counter-current heat exchanger located between the carotid arteries and the vessels which distribute blood to the brain. Basically what this means is that body heat is shunted away from the brain. While this protects the brain from overheating, the dog doesn't necessarily realise how hot its body is.

While raised a sheep dog, by the time Herks was old enough to work Joc and Stew had sold their sheep and taken on grazing cattle, so Herks became a good cattle dog instead.

Joc and Stew had chosen Herks because he was the fattest, greediest, ugliest pup in the litter of five – but those traits didn't last long. When talking about their boy they now describe his 'beautiful face and eyes, his soft woolly coat and his total trust in us.'

Herks was always wanting attention, and the way he got it was by talking and grunting and making all manner of noises. And whenever possible asking to shake hands with muddy paws. 'He had a big heart, was totally loyal and dedicated at all times and through all toughness.'

Mr Perkins Herkins' loyalty and big heart grew even more after retirement when he met a lovely lady called Cathy, who cared for him when his family was away. In fact, it could be called a crush. Herks loved Cathy, who had introduced this 'back of the truck' farm dog to the passenger seat and a cozy pet-style bed inside the house. Such was their new love that when Cathy would come to collect Herks for a sleep-over he would launch himself at the driver's door of her car – before it was actually opened.

Postscript

During the author's visit to meet Herks and his family, he fell ill and only a short time later sadly passed away. Hercules was deeply loved and is missed every day by his human family. This author was honored to meet such an amazing dog and to share a few of his last days, watching him enjoy his retirement lying under the beautiful white rose bushes.

As Joc and Stew remember, up until just before the end of 2012, Herks was the fittest most active dog. 'In his early retirement, he loved to go for long walks around Akaroa's hills and streets. He loved these walks and would become excited when he saw us put on our walking shoes and see his lead come out. He would spin around in circles, bark enthusiastically and try to grab the leash in his teeth. No barrier like a fence, however high, was ever a deterrent, stopping him getting from A to B. This agility came from his mother who was trained as a backing dog.

'When Herks became sick with what turned out to be bone cancer, his reluctance to jump the fence he had always jumped on our walks was the first indication something was wrong. As the disease advanced over the next few months, his wonderful energy was lost through the pain he suffered. One way he could communicate with us was to thump his big woolly tail where he lay, whenever he knew we were talking about him or to him or his name was mentioned! As you moved towards him the thumping increased in speed until he had you where he wanted . . . giving him a big pat, hug – anything for the contact. This was the last thing Herks did when Stew spoke his name as he passed away.'

Star dogs

Sparrow, Quinn and Audrey

Life on the streets is tough. No place for paws destined for stardom, but that's exactly where our star dogs started. Falling pregnant and giving birth to a litter of chihuahua mini fox terrier cross puppies, Mummy had to scavenge around local parks just to feed herself and find enough sustenance to feed her babies. Who knew what future lay ahead for these wee souls? Unbeknownst to this struggling mother, the universe had big plans for her tiny babies.

After being taken off the streets and into a foster home, life for Mummy and her pups would never be the same. From street life to stage lights, two of the puppies were destined for stardom. Their names, now seen in lights, are Sparrow and Quinn.

Dogs have worked in performance roles in film, television

and on stage for as long as the entertainment industry has been around, often stealing our hearts more than their human co-stars. Who can forget Old Yeller, Petey the pit bull terrier in *Little Rascals*, Toto in the *Wizard of Oz*, or Lassie and Rin Tin Tin? In fact, the original act-dog who played Rin Tin Tin was a shell-shocked German shepherd, rescued by an American serviceman during World War I, who went on to star in 23 Hollywood films.

Better known these days are *101 Dalmatians*, *Beethoven*, *Hachiko*, *Fang*, *Marley* and of course, Bruiser. Bruiser is one of the star dogs in *Legally Blonde*, and little Sparrow and Quinn were destined for the stage show of this movie.

They were discovered by chance when the dog trainer for the show, Peta Clarke, decided on a whim to visit the tiny six-week-old rescued street pups.

Renowned for their nervous dispositions, in the search to find the perfect performer, Peta had met many chihuahas. As Peta says, 'Searching for the right dog – one who not only looks the part, but can deal with everything that comes with working in theatre – is no mean feat. Confidence is essential, as is a quick bounce back when they get a spook. No dog is going to be totally confident in every situation, so you want a dog that when they do get a spook they get over it quickly. That's vital [for this job].'

The theatre, film and television environment for a working act-dog is far less natural than many other environments dogs work in, where they are called upon to maximise their natural senses and physical abilities.

In the entertainment industry, dogs are challenged mentally more than physically. They must be able to perform learned behaviours and remain focused in highly challenging situations, such as around the catering van!

When 'action' is called or the curtain goes up, acting dogs are expected to do their job without missing a beat along with their human co-stars. They must remain calm throughout the whole process even when there are lots of people around talking and yelling and then when they're not. When an orchestra is playing, actors warming up vocally and physically (no howling please), bright lights changing, huge curtains going up and down and when large cameras (scary eyes) are in their face. The dogs will be asked to repeat an action several times in a row and to do it on cue. All very demanding work.

Peta knew she had found the dog she was looking for when she first laid eyes on the runt of the street litter. She felt a rush of recognition and knew without doubt that this little boy, who would come to be known as Sparrow, had the makings of a great performer.

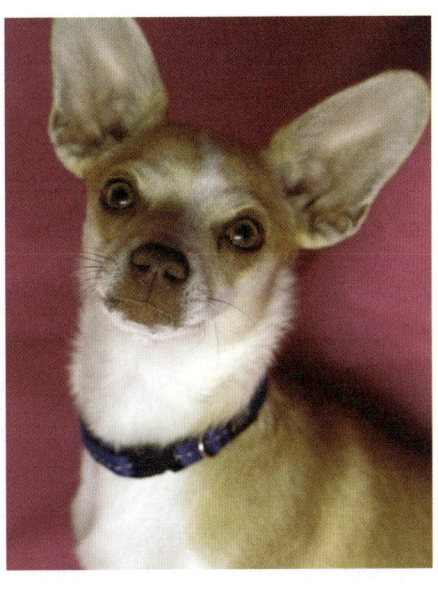

Quinn loves to improvise on stage.

But as any actor knows, each stage role requires an understudy, someone to do the show if the lead actor cannot. Sparrow's understudy would be his older brother, Quinn. It was Quinn who amused the audience during a show one night when he decided he'd been there, done that and it always ended the same way, so jumped out of the handbag he was in and ran off stage. In that particular scene the character, Bruiser, is meant to lie patiently in a handbag while the human actress holding it plays her part – not steal the show by jumping out and leaving the stage. On this occasion, however, she was forced to improvise quickly.

Peta knew the dogs wouldn't have a problem learning the 'show behaviours', so the more formal side of training was secondary at the beginning. First up she focused on building a strong emotional foundation for the puppies. Peta at the time was based in Brisbane where she was training and working the dogs in a production of *Annie*. 'The pups trotted in most days with the two doodles who were playing Sandy at the time, so there was lots of opportunity to get them feeling good about theatre. They were not only exposed to all the stimuli, they were

131

Sparrow, the star, sits patiently while his brother Quinn tries to hog the camera.

given the chance for these stimuli to be linked with the good stuff! There was lots of playing tug and eating roast chicken. If they didn't feel totally confident and comfortable in and around the theatre all the best training of the behaviours in the world would be pointless.'

Now, only a year old, the brothers are already veterans of the stage. They have over a hundred shows under their belts having performed eight shows a week for months on end. That's demanding on human actors, and for two-kilogram (4.4-lb) chihuahuas it's a big ask. They have done print interviews, television interviews and won the hearts of theatre patrons from all across Australia.

The pros can speak on cue, find their mark (designated place to stand), move from A to B when required and, yes, even sit in a handbag during the show in front of thousands of people.

From day one Sparrow exuded an inner calmness many humans strive to master. But being a practical joker, and a dog, Sparrow sometimes decides not to speak, forcing the actress he works with to do some very impressive and funny improvisations.

One night Sparrow stopped to sniff a pink feather boa on his way to jumping into the handbag and when he turned to face the audience he had a pink feather mo.

And at the end of the show it's fun time and anyone's best guess as to what they will do. Do they run on stage and take a bow, do they just run right past the actors and into the arms of their loving trainer who is waiting in the wings – they know she has better food waiting for them – or do they steal the show and just stay on stage bowing and bowing again?

Sadly, not long into the run, the bright lights would dim a little for Quinn. No, he hadn't been caught chasing a cat with his brother or tearing up the soft toys, and they had both started to grow out of their annoying humping behaviour – meaning Peta could finally read a book without her arm receiving their many advances. Rather unfortunately Quinn, Sparrow's best mate and partner in crime, had a couple of bad knees requiring surgery and months of rehabilitation (more work for Peta). On the bright side, once he is all healed, Quinn will once again be in the limelight, treading the boards.

Sparrow (Spaz) couldn't be expected to perform without an understudy, so once again Peta found herself the caregiver to a rescued nine-month-old chihuahua, Audrey, who's even smaller than the other two but 'big in attitude' and learning her lines super fast. You go, girl!

Water rescue dogs

Lela and Maisy

The International Life Saving Federation (ILS) defines a canine water rescue team as a qualified dog and handler who work as a unit assigned to protect life and safety on surf, non-surf and still-water beaches and at lakes or rivers.

But a situations vacant advertisement for this job may define it something more like:

Interested in saving lives and have the following qualifications? Must be over 12 months old and able to tow an inflatable boat with 20 people inside 3.5 kilometres back to shore using your mouth; must be prepared to jump from a helicopter hovering at 4.5 metres above the water's surface into raging seas; must enjoy speed boats and jumping from and climbing back aboard them. Must be able to rescue multiple unconscious people and deliver them safely to a waiting vessel or back to shore, deliver a tow line from boat to shore, search for a missing boat and if

134

Coached eagerly from the side by one of their own, a pack of water rescue dogs trains in the pool.

found tow it back to shore and help rescue any persons stranded under an upturned boat. Must be able to jump in and rescue people from a submerged car. Must enjoy working alone or as a team.

Desirable qualities – webbed feet, a strong jaw, oil- and water-resistant coat to prevent hypothermia, body large and strong enough to withstand rough seas (minimum 30 kilograms), established ability to swim for extended periods of time, often towing something or someone, and the graciousness to accept admiration and accolades for being a clever dog.

It's a very rigorous job description and, on top of all the skills these dog teams must have, there is up to three years' training in the water year-round before they even qualify as operational.

Who wouldn't want a magnificent dog like Lela coming to their rescue?

And a critical part of that training includes a 'call-off'. This is an extremely important action where the dog is asked to cease the action they are undertaking. A call-off can be made by the handler to the dog for protection of dog or the victim, the person doesn't need to be rescued anymore or the situation has changed and the dog must quit the action immediately and return to the handler.

The numerous benefits of water rescue dogs are obvious – speed, efficiency, strength, swimming skills, etc, especially for countries like Australia and New Zealand where much time is spent in and around the water, yet outside of Europe, and even then mainly Italy, they are a scarcity.

Roberto Gasbarri, who co-ordinates the Italian School of Canine Lifeguards programme, succinctly describes the benefits of water rescue dogs in an interview with the *Daily Mail*: 'Dogs are useful in containing the physical fatigue of the lifeguard, to

Maisy is a cute puppy now, and someday soon she'll be a grown-up rescue dog.

increase the speed at which casualties are retrieved, to increase the security of both the casualty and of the lifeguard.'

This is the reason why Phill Moore, trainer of and companion to water dogs Lela and Maisy, is determined to see his local New Zealand waters safer through the introduction of water rescue dogs.

In 2012 Phill and a handful of other likeminded lifesavers participated in the inaugural International Course for K9 Water Rescue Team Certificate implemented by the International Life Saving Federation, based in Belgium. The other 11 candidates came from the USA, Latvia, Ukraine, the UK, the Netherlands, Belgium and Finland. The dog Phill was working with was trained in Finnish, so he had to quickly add some new language skills to his repertoire. Until the ILS approved and implemented the K9 water rescue team certification, there was really only the one school for canine water rescue based in Italy. While water rescue by dogs isn't new, it's the newest form of rescue to be taught and certified.

Due to the nature of the work not many breeds would qualify as water rescue dogs and, while Labrador and golden retrievers also have an affinity with water, when it comes to water rescue most are Newfoundlands (Newfies).

Newfies were first discovered in Newfoundland, Canada, in the 1700s and have a documented history of search and rescue work. Males normally weigh between 60 and 70 kilograms (132 and 154 lb) and females 45 and 55 kilograms (99 and 121 lb), giving them the size and strength required for this work. The largest Newfy on record weighed 120 kilograms (264 lb) and measured over 1.82 metres (nearly 6 feet) from nose to tail.

Phill thinks possible reasons for a lack of water rescue teams in many countries is that Newfies aren't a common breed. Most are kept as pets or as show dogs, when in fact they were bred to be working dogs and help fishermen haul large nets. The commitment to training may be another obstacle. As with all search and rescue work, these volunteer teams must train all year round, in all weather, especially once they qualify as operational. And while training may start out with basic exercises, with the dog and handler running along the beach or swimming side by side for 200–300 metres (218–328 feet), it very quickly elevates to situations where the dog must recognise the difference between a decoy dummy and a real drownee and tow the genuine victim back to shore. They must also tow boats with or without people through all sorts of sea conditions to safety.

Phill says his first dog, Lela, loved the water, sometimes a little too much, and as a puppy they would joke that they should take her to Australia to find water for them because she would find any water anywhere to play in – and it didn't have to be clean! On- or off-duty Lela wanted to be in the water, or when off-duty and being a naughty dog, she loved chasing ducks across water from a great distance away . . .

Tragically Phill lost Lela at the young age of four. While she was alive, together they achieved the top working Newfoundland Award in the country for two years running, but sadly she passed away before she could be formally assessed as an operational water rescue dog. After all the hard work they had put in together, Phill says 'there was more to be learned by working with her and practising for rescue situations rather than just being able to perform the task required to pass a test'.

Phill has a new puppy now, Maisy, who will be in training to fill some rather large booties left by Lela and some rather large legends left by Newfies around the world over the past few centuries.

An unnamed Newfoundland is credited with saving Napolean Bonaparte in 1815 when he almost drowned by falling overboard while trying to escape exile on the island of Elba. It is believed a fisherman's dog jumped into the water and kept him afloat until he could reach safety.

In 1828 a Newfoundland named Hairyman helped his family save over 160 Irish immigrants from the wreck of the brig *Dispatch*.

And in the early twentieth century a Newfoundland saved 92 people, including an infant in a mailbag, who were on the SS *Ethie*, a boat wrecked off the northern peninsula of Newfoundland. The dog swam through turbulent waters in a blizzard and retrieved a rope from the boat and used it to bring everyone to shore – and safety.

EJ Pratt, who clearly loved dogs, commemorated this hero in the poem 'Carlo' published by the Canadian Forum, November 1920, and prefaced the same in an unnamed Newfoundland journal with 'The dog that saved the lives of over ninety persons in that recent wreck, by swimming with a line from the sinking vessel to the shore, well understood the importance as well as the risk of his mission.'

... I will fetch you with me when I die,
And standing up at Peter's wicket,
Will urge sound reasons for your ticket;
I'll show him your life saving label,
And tell him all about the cable,
The storm along the shore, the wreck,
The ninety souls upon the deck,
How one by one they came along
The young and old, the weak the strong,
Pale women sick and tempest-tossed,
With children given up for lost,
I'd tell him more, if he would ask it
How they tied a baby in a basket,
While a young sailor picked and able
Moved out to steady it on the cable;
And if he needed more recital
To admit a mongrel without title,
I'd get down low upon my knees
And swear before the Holy Keys,
That judging by the way you swam,
Somewhere within your line a dam
Formed for the job by God's own hand,
Had littered for a Newfoundland...

Animal assisted activity dogs

Panda

Panda and his owner, Lorraine Steele, visit a retirement home to offer emotional support, companionship and a good dose of oxytocin to all they meet, residents, staff and visitors alike.

Animal assisted activity dogs brighten the day and lift the spirits of people who are away from home for numerous reasons and who miss their own pets or purely and simply love dogs. The dogs act as motivators and often help these people set goals, even if that's just getting out of bed to see them.

Almost daily there are stories in the news about a sick or dying person comforted by the presence of a visiting dog. Petting the dog, letting the dog lie in bed with them, or even broaching conversation about dogs they had throughout their lives adds sparkle to the day for many elderly people in nursing homes. It is one such home that Panda visits every second week.

From the minute he was born on the cold concrete floor of a city pound, Panda and his 11 littermates were special. Each with

Above

As a puppy, Panda was always winning hearts.

Left

All grown up now, Panda also heals hearts.

their own unique personality, it became clear very quickly that Panda was going to be very laid-back, 'a lover not a fighter' as his human partner Lorraine describes him. So it was a foregone conclusion that with Lorraine's community spirit and Panda's easy-going, calm personality they would find a volunteer job which suited them both.

The residents at Onewa Lodge love Panda, and for some the news of his pending visit is all they need to leave their room or open their door. They all think he's a gentle giant, which he is with them. When he's on-duty there is no sign of the dog who chewed up the French leather boots, or redesigned the outside stairs when teething. The residents and staff never see a glimpse of the bull terrier/Great Dane/American bulldog cross who when off-duty leaps at any ball in any chucker in any human hand. No, he's an angel at work, who selflessly cleans up their afternoon tea crumbs and nestles in under a chair or bed for a quick nap between photoshoots with residents.

Whether in bed or in a wheelchair or sitting in front of the television, Panda's height (yes, he's tall) makes it easy for people to just reach out to pet him. And because he's such a handsome boy he wins hearts just by turning up.

But it's not just humans Panda helps. Because of his kind and generous nature Panda also helps dogs who have been rescued from all sorts of abuse learn to play and have fun again. On one such date, Panda clearly recognised that the girl dog visiting had no idea what to do in his presence, so he just lay his huge bulk down on the grass and gently pawed at her, at which point she mirrored him and the two never looked back.

Unfazed by almost everything in life except the hose and having a shower, when he doesn't have a doggie date or lots of humans to visit, Panda will entertain himself with anything that squeaks, smells like food, is food, swimming and sleeping.

Not that she's biased at all, but Lorraine describes Panda as 'the perfect man'!

Psychiatric service dogs and mental health therapy dogs

Dozer

Psychiatric service

As with all service dogs, psychiatric service dogs must be trained to perform at least three tasks which mitigate their human's mental health illness. These treasures also provide unlimited emotional support.

The ways a psychiatric service dog may help their humans often involves such duties as making them aware of and interrupting repetitive or injurious behaviours. They may also provide environmental assessment during times of uncertainty brought about by hallucinations, flashbacks or paranoia. During episodes such as flashbacks, which could be highly fraught for people before they had their service dog, people report that the presence of their dog can bring them back to the here and now.

A soldier having flashbacks said everything seemed so real during these episodes until his dog was there and some part of his brain was able to rationalise that his dog wasn't with him

144

in combat, so he must be at home having an episode, not still fighting.

Post traumatic stress disorder (PTSD) is an anxiety disorder which may develop as a result of a trauma. Symptoms include being vigilant or extra alert and aware of the environment, re-experiencing a traumatic experience through nightmares and/or flashbacks, and numbness in feelings.

There are numerous media articles on the help and hope dogs have given people with PTSD. The reasons given include the dogs delivering all the positive hormonal changes mentioned in the section on therapy dogs, and of particular benefit and interest is the increase in oxytocin.

To be a PTSD assistance dog, aside from the trained tasks the dog must demonstrate to qualify as a service dog, they have to be very calm, human-affectionate and display some degree of intelligent disobedience. Part of their role is to provide stability for the person with the disorder in the hope they may re-establish their ability to trust and feel love. At the same time, the animal provides reassurance that the person has a buddy with them, often allowing sleep and relief.

Edward O Wilson's 1984 biophilia hypothesis is based on the premise that our attachment to and interest in animals stems from the strong possibility human survival was partly dependent on signals from animals in the environment indicating safety or threat. The biophilia hypothesis suggests that now, if we see animals at rest or in a peaceful state, this may signal to us safety, security and feelings of well-being, which in turn may trigger a state where personal change and healing are possible.

There is currently much interest and research going into the efficacy of matching PTSD working dogs with returning soldiers suffering from PTSD. Aside from the aforementioned benefits, it is believed the dogs assist greatly in the process of their human reintegrating back into civilian life while still offering some of the structure of the military. For example, dogs thrive on routine and knowing their boundaries, they are as bonded to their humans as buddies in combat, they keep the person company and don't tell them to 'get it together' as other misguided but well-meaning humans may. The dogs never tire of the challenges involved in a disorder such as PTSD, they love their human anyway. The dogs keep people active and outdoors, by requiring care and attention which is contrary to self-involvement – and unwittingly garner social interaction.

Like medical response dogs, these psychiatric service dogs also remind people to take their medicine, retrieve items of assistance, and one of their most reassuring and endearing behaviours is to guide their human out of any situation, crowd or environment the person is finding stressful, to a safer place.

With their skills, these dogs can also be partnered with people with schizophrenia, anxiety or agoraphobia.

Mental health therapy

In a mental health therapy role, a dog such as Dozer can mean the difference between life and death for some people. One patient Dozer visited was on 24-hour suicide watch. She was in a very dark place in her life, at a time when she wanted to end it, but knowing Dozer was going to visit gave her something and she looked forward to it. When he visited it was the only time she would get out of bed. Not only would she get out of bed, she would smile and cuddle Dozer and talk to him – even if the big gallah was sitting on her foot, as is his custom when he recognises someone needs a little extra lovin'.

At 50 kilograms (110 lb), this English bulldog mastiff cross wins over many people who are afraid of dogs – and squashes a lot of toes while he's at it. Which many of the children he has worked with find very funny.

Before working with acute mental health patients, Dozer used to visit at-risk children who live in a secure residential unit. For many of those children, with sad family histories, meeting and spending time with Dozer was the first positive experience they'd ever had with a dog.

When not helping humans, Dozer helps his little brother Tana adjust to the world after a bad start to life.

Dozer's human, Maggie Butler, credits him with being the 'perfect therapy dog with an amazing ability to sense who needs him'. On a more personal note she says, 'We feel like we won the lottery with Dozer, he really is one in a million. I got him a few months after my precious mum passed away, and I always thought she found him for me because he really helped me deal with my grief of losing her.'

As well as helping Maggie with her grief, Dozer help his newly adopted brother Tana (not Montana; same name, different dog) when he came to live with them after an abusive start to life. Dozer assisted Tana in settling into a loving family, showed him the pleasures of soft toys, treats, living inside instead of outside on a chain, treats, walks at the park, treats, oh and more treats.

As beautiful as Dozer is, and as loving and affectionate as he may be, what all those he helps don't know is that he has a few dribbling and snoring issues.

Autism service dogs

Autism Spectrum Disorder (as defined by the *Merriam Webster Dictionary*) is:

> any of a group of developmental disorders (as autism and Asperger's syndrome) marked by impairments in the ability to communicate and interact socially and by the presence of repetitive behaviours or restricted interests – called also autistic spectrum disorder, pervasive developmental disorder.
>
> Autism: a variable developmental disorder that appears by age three and is characterized by impairment of the ability to form normal social relationships, by impairment of the ability to communicate with others, and by stereotyped behaviour patterns.

Worrisome behaviours for people with autism, or who have a child with autism include wandering/bolting/sneaking/escaping, pica (persistent and compulsive cravings to eat non-food items) self-harming, stimming (repetitive body movements, such as hand-flapping). Often these behaviours are brought on by anxiety, agitation, frustration and/or sensory overload. Because these behaviours can be so destructive to the individual and the people around them, vigilance is required in managing even the most basic day-to-day activities.

It's common for families living with a person with autism to experience a great amount of stress. The constant care and attention required to maintain a safe environment for the person, especially so for children, to address their education and to nurture socialisation, while also getting on with day-to-day life is extremely demanding and taxing.

Statistics show autism is one of the fastest-growing developmental diseases in the world, which in turn means more and more families are living under pressure. Thankfully, many families now have some respite by embracing a dog into their lives.

It has been less than 20 years since the first dogs were trained to assist children with autism, and their presence has been life-changing for many families.

Aside from being something the autistic child shows some interest in, a dog often encourages a non-verbal child to speak or make sounds, and provides valuable companionship.

Autism manifests differently for each individual, so the training dogs receive also differs, but one very common benefit is having a dog act as an 'anchor' to prevent a child from disappearing, bolting away or sneaking out the window at night. The dogs do this in two ways – by the therapeutic bond they develop with the child and by alerting parents. Allowing parents to actually get some sleep has been a godsend for these families.

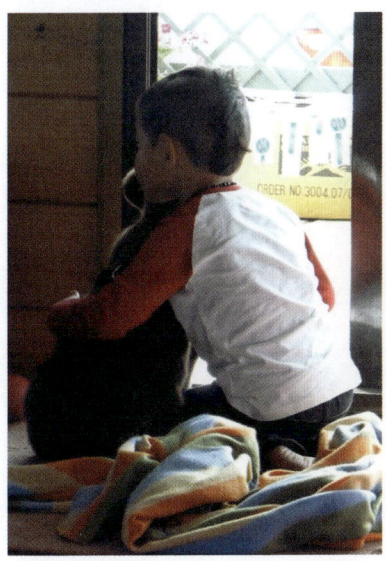

Anecdotal evidence suggests many children naturally gravitate towards the dogs. Most often when out walking, autistic children will hold the handle on the dog's jacket while another lead is also held by an adult and they won't leave the dog. This has the added advantage of preventing bolting.

A child with autism and his new assistance pup in training on their first day together.

If the child will walk next to the dog without stopping or stimming or trying to bolt, and will sit or play with the dog, this gives the child more independence as they don't have to have their hands held all the time by an adult. It's important to note that the autistic child is never left alone with the dog, there is always an adult present.

The dogs can interrupt dangerous behaviours such as self-harming or redirected aggression, pica and stimming.

Some of the dogs are trained in tracking or search and rescue, so the families have the peace of mind that, should the child somehow run away or disappear, the dog can track them down.

Another great thing these quiet, soft, compassionate dogs do for people with autism is calm them in times of a meltdown, seizure or nightmare by laying on the person's lap or applying firm pressure or even by just giving old-fashioned affection and licking the person.

Other assistance includes scent detection for certain food items a child may not be allowed to eat, such as gluten or peanuts, guiding the child in difficult social situations or around obstacles, and providing counter-balancing if needs be.

While most people may hear a fire alarm and know what to do, for a person with autism the same alarm may prove to be far too overwhelming and they may not know how to respond or may respond inappropriately. Here again a dog can act as a safety manager, leading the child or person to safety.

With all the wonderful ways a dog can help someone with autism, more and more autistic children are able to integrate into 'normal' life and have friends and some form of social life. While their caregivers can never completely relax their vigilance, at least the dogs provide some priceless peace of mind.

Conclusion

History shows us that dogs have been engaged in assisting humans in warfare, travel and discovery for millennia. But it was only in the last half of the twentieth century that working with dogs became a serious business or rather dogs were taken more seriously. Aside from the growing number of scientific studies and enormous mass of anecdotal evidence, dogs themselves have proven time and time again to be reliable, dedicated, credible assistants in all areas of humanity from warfare to welfare and everywhere in between – science, medicine, education, entertainment and rehabilitation.

From tracking poachers across the great African reserves to digging for avalanche survivors on the snow-covered slopes of Switzerland, from sniffing out endangered whale poop in the North Atlantic to finding lost families in the South Pacific, from leading the blind in Australia to undertaking scientific research in Thailand, from detecting hidden explosives in war-torn Afghanistan to assisting the elderly and ill in New Zealand, the dogs in this book, and many more like them, are doing these jobs every day all around the world.

A well-deserved treat for Savannah.

Yet it's a tragedy that millions of dogs are still abandoned and sitting in shelters or living on the streets while their potential and desire to help us and make the world a better place goes unseen and untapped. While researching for this book I was amazed at the number and variety of jobs that dogs have. Some are still in early trial stages, while others are quietly taking place in the far corners of the globe – fighting the multi-billion-dollar pirated DVD business, instigating a change in law by the Sharia Council to allowed guide dogs in public places owned by Muslims, fighting the battle against arsonists with accelerant detection dogs, finding lost pets by using working dogs to track them … the list goes on.

The ways in which dogs can help humans appears to be limited only by our imaginations, our understanding of their nature, the progress of science and our ability to harness their natural skills.

The road for dogs over the course of history has not been smooth or shiny. Despite all their hard work and loyalty, dogs have not yet received the recognition they deserve – not by a long way. It is my deepest hope that this book will open people's eyes to the phenomenal range of tasks dogs take on and master, and will give these animals the respect and appreciation they deserve. Dogs are far more than pets, far more than we give them credit for, far more than we are capable of understanding: they are truly extraordinary.

> But the poor Dog, in life the firmest friend,
> The first to welcome, foremost to defend,
> Whose honest heart is still his Master's own,
> Who labours, fights, lives, breathes for him alone,
> Unhonoured falls, unnoticed all his worth,
> Denied in heaven the Soul he held on earth –
> While man, vain insect! hopes to be forgiven,
> And claims himself a sole exclusive heaven.
>
> *Epitaph to a Dog* (Lord Byron, 1808)

Glossary

AAA   The general 'meet and greet' activities which involve pets visiting people.

AAT   A goal-directed intervention in which progress is measured and documented. A health professional will direct AAT as a normal part of their practice.

Adoption   To take into one's family.

Air scent dog   A search dog, which attempts to find a lost subject by locating the cone of airborne scent emitted by the person.

Alert   Term used for physical signs a canine gives when they are interested in something or have found the source for which they have been searching. Canines may alert by barking, sitting or any other trained behaviour.

Avalanche   Defined in dictionaries as a mass of snow, rock, and ice falling down a mountain. In practice the term avalanche refers to a snow avalanche unless the words rock, ice, mud, etc, are specifically used.

Back country   The area beyond mid-country access. More than four hours' walking distance of a vehicle-navigable road/ track or trail head.

Call-out   The executive command to mount an operation whereby all personal are required to deploy.

Dog team   One handler and one canine.

FEMA   Federal Emergency Management Agency (in the USA).

Fine search   A directed search where the search grids are close together.

First responder   A person trained in the medical and mechanical skills and knowledge necessary to successfully manage the initial care of an individual until the person can either be evacuated or placed under more intense care. The term 'first responder' is usually associated with police, fire, and ambulance response in the non-SAR environments.

GPS   Global (or ground) positioning system. Based upon satellites, this small computer will give exact locations using latitude and longitude.

Handler   The person who controls and directs a canine during a search. This person is usually, but does not have to be, the owner or trainer of the canine.

Hasty search   A search whose purpose is to cover the most obvious places a subject might be in the least time possible. Usually the first kind of search tactic to be utilised.

Hypothermia   A generalised cooling which may lower the body temperature below normal, and if untreated may prove fatal.

Incident   An occurrence or event, whether human-caused or natural phenomena, requiring action by emergency service personnel to prevent or minimise loss of life or damage to property and/or natural resources.

Indicate   *see* Alert.

Mission   A specific incident such as a search and rescue operation.

Perimeter search   A search of an outside line believed to be across the direction of travel of the subject. The objective is to cut the trail and find tracks or other evidence of the subject having been there.

PTSD   Post traumatic stress disorder.

Rappel   To descend a rope at a safe, controlled speed.

Recovery, body   The retrieval of human remains following a fatal incident.

Rescue An operation to retrieve people in distress, provide for their initial medical or other needs, and deliver them to a place of safety.

SAR Search and rescue.

Search A formal search involves assembling, co-ordinating and using the necessary resources to find lost, stranded, trapped or injured people, to save lives or avoid further injury.

Speak Training word used to cue a dog to vocalise on command.

Track A physical impression left from the passage of a person or an animal.

Tracking canine A search dog able to follow the ground scent of a person who has passed through an area in which the dog is searching.

Trailing canine A search dog able to follow the scent trail of a specific individual, after the dog has been allowed to smell an article or object which has been in contact with the individual. The trailing dog is scent-discriminating (has the ability to distinguish and follow the scent of one person).

Urban SAR (USAR) The act of searching for and/or rescuing people from collapsed buildings. These situations are characterised by extensive rubble, movement of heavy debris and the extrication of trapped people, and may follow an earthquake or explosion.

Wilderness/Land SAR A search and rescue mission conducted in an uncultivated and uninhabited area, often inaccessible by road.

Wind chill The physical temperature felt by a body when the actual temperature is lowered by gusts of wind.

References and contacts

Research for this book has been done in the field with dogs and their families and/or handlers, and online, through numerous books and by conversations with professionals. For more information about dogs in particular jobs, here are some contact details that may be of assistance.

Key books of interest

Practical Guide for Sporting and Working Dogs by Dominique Grandjean, Nathalie Moquet, Sandrine Pawlowiez, Anne-Karen Tourtebatte, Boris Jean and Hélène Bacqué. Royal Canin Group, France, 2000.

Saving Private Sarbi by Sandra Lee. Allen & Unwin, Sydney, 2011.

Inside of a Dog by Alexandra Horowitz. Simon & Schuster, New York, 2009.

In Defence of Dogs by John Bradshaw. Penguin, London, 2011.

Training the Disaster Search Dog by Shirley M Hammond. Dogwise Publishing, Washington, 2006.

The Intelligence of Dogs by Stanley Coren. Simon & Schuster, London, 2006.

Doglopaedia by JM Evans and Kay White. Henston, UK, 1985.

The Dogs of War by Lisa Rogak. St Martin's Press, New York, 2011.

Internet contacts

Search and Rescue

International Rescue Dog Association: www.iro-dogs.org/en.html

Search and Rescue Dogs: searchdogs.co.nz

NZ USAR Association: www.usardogs.org.nz

Zermatt Matterhorn: www.zermatt.ch

Search and Rescue Dogs Australia: www.sarda.net.au

Australian Swiss Search Dog Association Inc:
www.assda-sardogs.org.au

SAR Dogs Tasmania: www.sardogstasmania.org.au

National Association of Search and Rescue USA: www.nasar.org

Search and Rescue Dog Association UK:
www.sardaengland.org.uk

Swiss Search and Rescue: www.swiss-sar.ch

Search and Rescue Stories: www.sarstories.com

National Service Dogs Canada: www.nsd.on.ca

Thai Rescue Dog Association: www.thai-rda.org

Service dogs

Australia

A.W.A.R.E. Dogs Australia Inc: www.awaredogs.org.au

Canine Helpers for the Disabled Inc: www.caninehelpers.org.au

Assistance Dogs Australia: www.assistancedogs.org.au

Smart Pups: www.smartpups.org.au

New Zealand

Perfect Partners Assistance Dogs Trust: www.ppadt.org.nz

Mobility Assist Dogs Trust: www.mobilitydogs.co.nz

Assistance Dogs NZ Trust: assistancedogstrust.org.nz

New Zealand Epilepsy Assist Dogs Trust:
www.epilepsyfoundation.org.nz/assist-dog-trust

Assistance Animals Aotearoa: Kotuku Foundation

Other

Assistance Dogs International:
  www.assistancedogsinternational.org

International Association of Assistance Dog Partners (IAADP):
  www.iaadp.org

For a list of organisations around the world, visit
  www.iaadp.org/whoswho.html

Therapy dogs

Australia

Delta Society: www.deltasocietyaustralia.com.au

Therapy Dog Associations in Australia

The Australian Directory of Human Animal Interaction
  programmes: www.humananimalinteraction.org.au

New Zealand

Canine Friends Pet Therapy: www.caninefriends.org.nz

St Johns Outreach Therapy Pets: www.stjohn.org.nz

Therapy Dogs International: www.tdi-dog.org

Other

The Mira Foundation: www.mira.ca

International Society for Autism Research: www.autism-insar.org

Medical Detection Dogs: www.medicaldetectiondogs.org.uk

Cancer Dogs Canada: www.cancerdogs.com

InSitu Foundation: www.dogsdetectcancer.org

Pine Street Foundation: www.pinestreetfoundation.org

International Guide Dog Federation: www.igdf.org.uk

Royal NZ Foundation of the Blind: www.rnzfb.org.nz

Guide Dogs Australia: www.guidedogsaustralia.com

Seeing Eye Dogs Australia: www.seda.org.au

International Hearing Dog Inc: www.ihdi.org

Hearing Dogs NZ: www.hearingdogs.org.nz

Lions Hearing Dogs Australia: www.hearingdogs.asn.au

Hearing Dogs for Deaf People: www.hearingdogs.org.uk

**To see more of the dogs in this book
you can visit them online at:**

Drake
   http://www.dvidshub.net/video/279336/sgt-garrett-grenier

Gemma
   German shepherd puppy – Gemma – YouTube
   Search & Rescue Dog – Gemma – YouTube

Lennox
   Lennox the Red Nose Pitbull – Facebook

Rocket
   Aspiring Avalanche Dogs– NZ Documentary – YouTube

Roselle
   Roselle911 GuideDog – Facebook

Rocky and Jerry
   Big Life Foundation – Facebook

Savannah
   K9SARLog – Facebook
   ThaiRDA – Facebook
   K9savannah – YouTube

Acknowledgements

I have had the most fantastic time working on this project! I have met amazing dogs, had the most awesome experiences and learnt a phenomenal amount about what is going on in the canine world, more than I could fit in one book. Thank you to everyone for being so incredibly receptive.

I am in awe of, and eternally grateful to, all of the human partners of the dogs I have interviewed. They have been unbelievably generous with their time and knowledge, and most of all with their dogs. Thank you! To meet such a dedicated group of people who love and respect their dogs has been uplifting and inspiring.

It has been wonderful dealing with people who have incredible dogs themselves, yet talk so respectfully about other working dogs, as if their own jobs were a comparative breeze – you are amazing.

I began this project with a great adventure. Managing my fear of heights, claustrophobia and the cold, I participated in a training session, which saw me buried in a snow cave, and then fulfilled a life's dream by mushing a dog sled. It was the perfect start to this book – huge thanks to Matt, and to Kitty for sharing how things are done in Switzerland.

Ray and Dianne and the team at the NZ Sled Dog Festival – massive thanks. I didn't even mind getting up at 4am to see the sun rise over the mountains, bringing with it a Sun Dog – how perfect! Awesomeness brought to life. Thank you so much for sharing your wealth of knowledge with me and assisting along this journey. Mushing your dogs was one of the most incredible things I have ever done – it was a dream come true and I want to do it again! Arluk, when you came to me for a snuggle I felt blessed beyond belief – thank you. Blaze, you incredible girl, I am in awe. Thank you Lyne, for sharing Blaze.

Graeme, you have been a fountain of knowledge, and it has been so exciting following your adventures and seeing Odin qualify over the course of this project. Thank you for being so helpful with fact checking. You're far too modest, our communities need more people and dogs like you, Gemma and Odin.

Karen as always, you're a whiz. Thank you for your help, expertise and the intros. I'm disappointed Jet didn't pass his truffle training and that we can't join you.

Peta, you're an inspiration, mentor and all-round fabulous animal person. Thank you for everything.

Joc and Stew, I'm so pleased your special boy gets to live on in this book. I feel privileged I was able to share a few days with Mr Hercules and a huge thank you for sharing at such a difficult time.

Dogs brought us together, Maggie, and I'm so pleased. Dozer, you were very brave letting me get a few pics because it was obvious you didn't like the camera and I did my best not to upset you.

Claire and Mike, Vicki and Jenna, thank you for allowing me to include your wonderful dogs in this book, they make it complete.

Celia, the whole team thank you for your gracious and generous contribution in sharing Kiri with us at a very difficult time, thank you.

Phill, I wish you all the success in the world, we need those water rescue dogs! Thank you for sharing Lela and cute little (big) Maisy.

Justin, just in time! I loved meeting Jip.

Melanie, your dogs always inspire me and thank you for being so enthusiastic and happy to help. I had the best time in Bangkok with Savannah and Zambezi; thank you Sue and Andy for being so generous with your time and knowledge and girls. And much appreciation for the collars you donated.

Lorraine, I am so thrilled to have Panda in this book – thank you again for your support, your belief in me, your endless encouragement and for the genesis of a book like this.

Belinda, I cannot thank you enough for everything you have done. The hours and hours you spent explaining and editing and making sure I understood the nuances of service and therapy dogs. From a ropey bus ride to a hospital bed and everywhere in between, you have been amazing! Thank you, thank you, thank you, for your commitment, introductions and enthusiasm. And Tana, you're a diamond amongst dogs, you know exactly when to tell a girl it's time to go get some chocolate.

Don, Brett, Andrew and Philip, thank you for all the support and the enthusiasm you have had for the project. I really appreciate your help and enjoyed a good laugh as well.

To Sgt Grenier and Drake, kia kaha. Thank you for being who you are and doing what you do and for being part of the incredible pack of dogs in this book. May you and all your fellow soldiers always come home safe.

Much appreciation to Senior Sergeant Pedersen – we got there in the end. I extend my a huge thanks to the supportive and encouraging team at the Police Dog Section in Auckland and to Sergeant Salmond and Officer Jess for the incredible work you do. Officer-to-be Zeus and Senior Constable Evans, we should do it again sometime, it was a blast and you all know why!

To Eric from Ndarakwai Ranch, and Damien from Honeyguide Foundation and Big Life Foundation, thank you for being so willing to participate in my book and for being so helpful and communicative from so far away. Elephants are a life's passion of mine and I am thrilled to share with the world these amazing dogs working to help conserve this precious, precious endangered species.

Fiona, your feedback was as valuable as ever, I'm glad you're as crazy about working dogs as I am. Flip, years ago when you told me Jet could be much better than a 'Wonder Dog', you really set the ball rolling and inspired me, a massive thank you for that and everything else.

Oliver, thank you. Your endless patience with my crazy vet-related questions, requests for advice and your willingness to help me however you can is greatly appreciated! To you, Richard, Cheryl and the whole team at Onewa Road Vet Clinic, it's unanimous in our house: you're the best.

Quinny, you've waited so long and always been so encouraging, finally here it is! Jan and Adrian, thanks for the support and hospitality. Steve and Liz, thanks for the intros. Thanks also to Jon and Linda for helping in the rush.

Jesse, it was very sweet the way you sat by me all day when I was writing, but not so sweet when you sat on me – it's very hard to type with a golden retriever giving you a body hug. And Lulu, well Lulu didn't really care what I was doing unless she wanted me to be doing something she wanted to do, then she let me know.

Jet, my boy, you have again shown great patience with my endless staring at this white machine, covering your eyes or removing yourself quietly to the spare bed late at night when the light was still on. Your communication skills are fantastic and entertaining to say the least. You may be a challenge at times, but you make me strive to be a better dog person and I love you for that and everything else. You're my buddy.

Peter, a million thanks for making sure my boy is safe and sound while I go off to play with other dogs.

To Ian Watt and Exisle Publishing, thank you for all this.

To the great Dr Ian Dunbar, for everything you have done, are doing and will do for dogs in this world, all canids, their companions and I owe you a huge debt of gratitude. Thank you for being you and for loving dogs the way you do.

Lastly, but by no means least, to my grandfather for the advice from which I have never wavered: 'Never trust a man who doesn't like dogs', and to my mum who also loves dogs, thank you!

Photo acknowledgements

The author is grateful to everyone who supplied photographs for this book:

New Zealand Police: pp. 25, 26, front cover.

Belinda Simpson: pp. 37, 44, 147.

Jenna Reid-Batchelor: p. 43.

Claire and Mike Webb: pp. 48, 49.

Vicki Sheen: p. 54.

Celia King: pp. 57, 58.

Kitty Gilli: pp. 69, 72.

Graeme Hill: pp. 76, 79.

Rob Sinclair: p. 81.

Big Life Foundation: pp. 85, 87, 88.

Sgt Christopher Bonebrake (US Army) and Garrett Grenier:
    pp. 109, 110, front cover.

New Zealand Customs Service: pp. 113, 115.

Peta Clarke: pp. 131, 132.

Phill Moore: pp. 135, 136, 137.

Fiona Tomlinson: back cover.

Other photographs are from the author's collection.

Index